# Curse of the
# MEN-IN-BLACK
## Return of the UFO Terrorists

### Includes The
### Rare Classic
### THE UFO WARNING

# By John Stuart and
# Timothy Green Beckley

## GLOBAL COMMUNICATIONS

# Curse of the Men in Black
# Return of the UFO Terrorists

## by Timothy Green Beckley

### with
### Nick Redfern, John Stuart, Sean Casteel, Andrew Lunn, ATarrC

Timothy Green Beckley: Editorial Director
Carol Rodriguez: Publishers Assistant
Tim Swartz: Associate Editor
Sean Casteel: Editorial Assistant
Cover Art: Tim R. Swartz

For free catalog write:
**Global Communications**
**P.O. Box 753**
**New Brunswick, NJ 08903**

**Free Subscription to Conspiracy Journal E-Mail Newsletter**
**www.conspiracyjournal.com**

# Contents

UFO Silencers: They Have Not Gone Away!  by Timothy Green Beckley ............... - 7 -

UFO Warning by John Stuart ................................................................ - 11 -

Return Of The Men In Black by Timothy Green Beckley ...................... - 87 -
   Timothy Beckley Goes On The Trail Of The  Dreaded Men-In-Black
   With The UFO Hunters by Sean Casteel ............................................ - 87 -
   Another Strange Case Collected by Robert Goreman ........................ - 96 -

Men in Black... Real Life Cookie Monsters! by ATarrC ........................ - 97 -
   Men In Black Terrorize Witnesses In Calama ................................ - 98 -

Mothmen and Men in Black ............................................................. - 99 -

They've Come To Take You Away ..................................................... - 105 -
   Men In Black In Phoenix ............................................................. - 106 -
   MJB and A Black Helicopter ....................................................... - 108 -

MJBs, UFOs, and the Carlos Allende Letters ..................................... - 111 -

Horrific Unseen Forces ................................................................ - 123 -

Exploring The MJB Flap In UK by Andrew Lunn .............................. - 135 -
   Part 1: The Making of the Myth ................................................. - 135 -
   Part 2: Common Characteristics of the Modern Day MJB ................ - 136 -
   Part 3: MJB & Black Helicopters ................................................ - 138 -

The Mib and the World of Anne Henson by Nick Redfern ..................... - 141 -

Are The Mib  Killing Our Ufo Researchers? by Prof. G. Cope Schellhorn .......... - 145 -
   Phil Schneider ......................................................................... - 145 -
   Ron Rummel ............................................................................. - 147 -
   Ron Johnson ............................................................................. - 147 -

Ann Livingston ............................................................ - 148 -

Karla Turner ............................................................... - 149 -

Danny Casolaro ........................................................... - 149 -

Mae Bussell ............................................................... - 150 -

Deck Slayton .............................................................. - 150 -

Brian Lynch ............................................................... - 150 -

Capt. Don Elkin ........................................................... - 150 -

Bizarre Death of Scientists ............................................. - 150 -

Jessup and McDonald ..................................................... - 152 -

Dorothy Kilgallen ........................................................ - 152 -

Dr. James McDonald ....................................................... - 153 -

Astronomer M.K Jessup .................................................... - 153 -

Frank Edwards ............................................................ - 154 -

Ivan T. Sanderson ........................................................ - 155 -

The Mysterious Life and Death of Philip Schneider By Tim Swartz With
    assistance from Cynthia Drayer ................................... - 157 -

Railroad Cars ............................................................ - 158 -

"Star Wars" And The Alien Threat" ....................................... - 159 -

Black Helicopters ........................................................ - 159 -

Terrorist Bombings ....................................................... - 159 -

Something Looks Strange My Friend Compiled By Robert Goreman ............. - 164 -

Abduction Researcher Karla Turner  The Men In Khaki by Greg Bishop ........ - 165 -

The Guardian Men In Black, An Investigation Subject Bob Oechsler .............. - 167 -

Biographical Information Sheet - Bob Oechsler ............................ - 172 -

Guardian Investigation – The UFO Video Case ............................. - 173 -

The Insiders Report By Bob Oechsler ..................................... - 175 -

Preliminary Conclusions ................................................. - 180 -

The Field Investigation .................................................. - 181 -

Some Final Conclusions ................................................... - 185 -

The Aftermath ............................................................ - 186 -

Vanishing MIB – Ghosts Or Teleportation? By Tim Swartz .................. - 189 -

Smile MIB – Your On "Candid Camera" ..................................... - 197 -

# UFO SILENCERS: THEY HAVE NOT GONE AWAY! BY TIMOTHY GREEN BECKLEY

## An Update On The Notorious Men In Black

Millions watched the episode of the **UFO Hunters** titled **The Silencers** in which I detailed my own encounter with a real man in black. Shown to an national audience for the first time, was a photograph I took back in the 1960s of a strangely dressed individual who was standing in the doorway of a research associate of mine. Along with Jim Moseley, a long time UFOlogist who was than publishing a magazine **Saucer News**, I had driven from Manhattan to Jersey City to the apartment building where Jack and Mary Robinson said they were being stalked by a typical MIB who was watching their in home office and listening in on their phone conversations. Some of their files were even reported missing. Jim and I wanted to see for ourselves if such a sinister individual was actually lurking in the neighborhood. The entire story is told in my previous book **UFO Silencers: The Mysterious Men In Black**. The volume is available on Amazon.com or through the bookstore of our own **www.ConspiracyJournal.com** web site. And while I had more or less pushed thoughts of the MIB out of my mind, satisfied to spend my research time on other projects, my appearance on the History Channel opened up a whole new can of worms, when I began to receive both new and older reports which had never been disseminated to those investigators who take such accounts seriously. This book is an effort to put together a great deal of the material I have gathered since my early book on the MIB. One of the most chilling encounters that reached my attention came via an e mail only a few months ago. We reprint it word for word

\* \* \* \* \*

Beckley, sometime ago I purchased your book on the Men in Black. I've always been hugely interested in the MIB and it always made my skin crawl to think these things are out there.

About six months ago my friend Linda visited Albany Rural Cemetery in Menands, NY, supposedly haunted. She drove her car up a hill, the cemetery is a massive city of the dead, with many twisting and turning roads, large mausoleums and shadowy areas, very scarey!

Anyway, she went over there to go on a historical tour. It contains the bodies of Pres. Chester Arthur, illustrious Albany, NY historical figures like mayors and governors and Charles Fort! I need not explain to you who that was.

Up the hill she went and around a curve. She stopped. The day was a very nice one sunny and warm but those little milk weeds were blowing in the air and her car was covered with them from the field next to the grave yard. She had the windows down and if anyone was approaching she would have heard. The roads are gravel and the sound of tires coming up the hill would have been heard.

As she pulled over to stop, she was astounded by a MASSIVE black SUV, almost looked military like, so close behind her it could have parked in her rear seat! NO milk weed was on the car, but it was shiny and new looking, like they had just pulled out of the showroom. She didn't hear a thing, it made no sound at all.

Linda, who is a fan of the unknown, like me very slowly put the car in forward and crept forward, waiting to see if the SUV would follow. The windows were completely black and she had a very strange feeling from the thing. It didn't go after her, but backed up and Linda watched it go down one of the side roads that would take you back to the main entrance on Broadway.

She followed it! *ONLY THERE WAS NO ROAD WHERE THE SUV DISAPPEARED INTO*, only a chain link fence!!! She went back down the hill the way she came in and the thing was parked next to the office in the middle of the road, "like they were waiting for me". She slowly pulled up next to it and saw a man all in black, strange looking, standing next to the drivers' window like he was talking. Only the window was up. Linda gunned the car, watching all the time in the rear mirror and the man disappeared! Just blinked out. GONE.

This really got me going, so I went online to see what it said about the cemetery, and lo and behold the cemetery is haunted by vanishing black vehicles, mysterious men in black, a big black dog and a couple who fly over the headstones at dusk in their pajamas!

Two weeks later, still thinking about this and quite excited by it, I went to the Delmar Plaza with my mother to a dollar store. As I got back in the car we noticed a really big black SUV next to us. I joked that it must be the vehicle Linda saw, only the windows were down and it looked pretty normal inside. BUT around from the back came this creepy little man *ALL IN BLACK*.

He looked like that picture you have in your book only he had a black leather cap on, short sleeved black shirt that looked brand new, black pants, black shoes and black sox and black glasses. As I watched him he walked in front of our car and very deliberately turned slowly and looked at me with a smile that was a kind of knowing smile like, "Yes, here I am". I really believe it was an MIB. I should have followed him or waited to see where he went but we left.

My neice lives in an apt. building with one of the caretakers at the cemetery and he confirmed that he's heard all the stories, but has never actually seen anything himself.

Anyway, that's my story, and it's all true, Mr. Beckley. Just wanted to let you know the MIB are still active in the Albany, New York area. Claudia Cunningham, Glenmont, NY

* * * * *

Of course there are many, many stories to relate as told by seemingly reliable witnesses and researchers from the four corners of the globe.

In fact, one of our ultimate realizations early on in our investigation of UFOs and those who try to keep unfathomable, dark secrets about the phenomenon, is that we must think of this mystery as truly global in nature and not just confined to America and its complacent allies such as Canada and Great Britain. In fact, if anything, these just mentioned nations seem to huddle together in their agreement to keep this all under military and economic raps for the benefit of big business and the armed forces. Some feel the MIB might well be working for the economic industrial complex or at least are in agreement to squelch any evidence that would bring great advancement to our planet. It could well be that the MIBs are cronies of the darkest elements of our society who would like to keep enlightenment away from earth's general populace.

To begin our trip we must enter our time machine (you mean you don't have one?) and go back a few decades almost to the very beginning of organized UFO research and the silencing of one of the key investigators of the that period. John Stuart was in the early 1950s a "top dog" in UFOlogy in the land down under. He was interviewing witnesses and filing reports and had started a branch of Albert K Bender's International Flying Saucer Bureau. Both men got into "trouble" at about the same time as the Men In Black came from their invisible perch to issue their threats to stop all investigation of the flying saucers and the discussion of where they might originate from and how they are propelled. The warnings were serious issue – the threats certainly so deadly – that both men despite their status among their peers closed down their groups immediately.

Jim Moseley editor of Saucer Smear has said, "In its own unique way, John Stuart's *UFO Warning* is arguably the best flying saucer book ever written..."

It has been out of print for years, but in our attempt to provide today's researchers with valuable collectibles from the past, we have decided to include the entire text of this manuscript originally issued by our friend Gray Barker's Saucerian Press. Despite its "sensitive" nature we have not done any editing, and have decided to leave in even the most terrifying report of a mortifying rape at the hands of diabolical creatures. Let this be a warning of what could happen to you!

Tim Beckley photographed on the set of UFO Hunters as they go
about shooting the episode The Silencers where he got to show
the photo he took of what appears to be an
authentic Man in Black.

# UFO
# WARNING

## By JOHN STUART

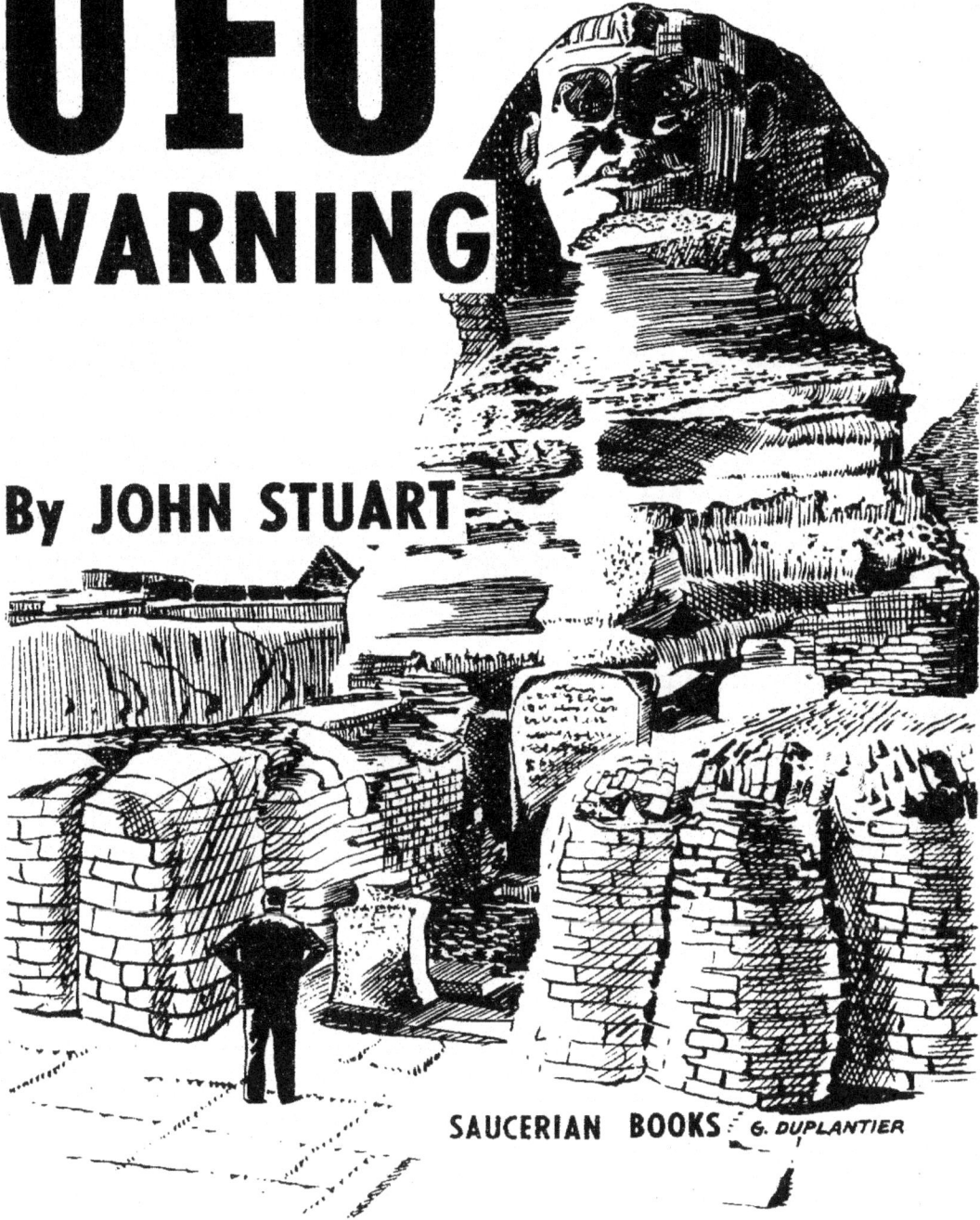

SAUCERIAN BOOKS  G. DUPLANTIER

I would like to record my sincere gratitude Gray Barker for the assistance he gave me during period Flying Saucer Investigators operated. In the New Zealand idiom, Gray was always, and still is, a "fair dinkum cobber." He stuck by me as a sincere friend when my own countrymen who were investigators and researchers deserted me, refusing to accept my word that I had known some strange experiences.

Never once did he question my word, nor refused to accept my data without having the absolute physical proof which I could not give him.

If, in the publication and the printing of my manuscript, Gray sticks out his neck out too far and gets it chopped off, I shall be truly sorry -- but not dismayed. For, as he has been capable of doing in the past, he will only grow a longer one.

**John Stuart**
**Hamilton, New Zealand**
**1963**

# INTRODUCTION

**Most** readers of this volume will have known of John Stuart through the reading of my own book, *They Knew Too Much About Flying Saucers* (University Books, 1956).

He was one of the researchers, which I told about, who had been "hushed," (using popular Ufological terminology) after finding out what was perhaps too much about Flying Saucers. In my book I recorded the explanation that John furnished me at that time.

As this volume will develop, I was unable to present the actual facts of the matter as John now writes them, because he felt it necessary at that time to mislead me a little so that his information had some chance of being believed.

In this respect he acted no differently than did Albert K. Bender, who, in his recent volume, *Flying Saucers and the Three Men*, honestly admits that he misled many people in order to protect himself. I believe that anybody who reads this volume by Stuart and Bender's book will instantly forgive these researchers for a bit of deception which they felt was tremendously important while they were in danger.

What you are about to read is, to me, a far more shocking account than you read in Al Bender's book. It is a book which is unpleasant for me to publish. It is a book which is unpleasant for you to read. But it is a book which neither I the publisher, nor you the reader, can overlook. Nor censor. Nor hide somewhere with the hope that nobody will read it and be warned by it.

John Stuart's unpleasant experiences were not presented to you in this form until after we had given the matter of its publication a great deal of thought. I think that the decision to publish it came from the innate and irrepressible instincts of a reporter rather from the sound judgment of a commercial publisher.

Although I cannot completely understand this volume, and I doubt if many others can either, it is a definite part of the huge mass of confusing data which has so far formed the UFO enigma. It may be helpful to others, who possess a greater understanding than do I, and assist them in uncovering hidden facets of the Flying Saucer Mystery.

In its rawest and most primary sense it will serve as a warning to many UFO students, since it will inform them that within the framework of the Enigma exists pitfalls which can cause grief and danger. I would not want this book to construe however, the idea that everybody should give up UFO research because there are evidently certain negative areas involved, which can be tapped and unleashed, causing great pain.

Those who are as familiar as am I with the field of flying saucers know decisively of the frustrating inability we have experienced in obtaining and offering incontrovertible physical proof of the existence of such objects. This we have tried to do, without a complete understanding of why we have tried it. So far I think we can be highly satisfied, however, with the by-products of this frustrating quest.

To a materialist, which I represent, such by-products are not hard to demonstrate in a physical sense. Higher than the possibility of life on other worlds, physical and spiritual assistance from space people, I value the friends I know, personally, and by correspondence, whom I have gained through the pursuit of this subject.

Other people, I am quite certain, can look deeper into these by-products, and find non-material values which may likewise transcend actual proof or solution to the mystery.

What I have gained, I do know, has been of a positive nature. In the logical expression of a universe, however, there must exist, also, negative influences.

This volume, most capably, expresses such. As a part of the definitive literature on this subject, this work also becomes a responsibility, literarily speaking. Its interpretation will also be varied and hotly argued. Perhaps some sort of a definite conclusion can be reached after it is widely read and discussed, yet I doubt it.

An understanding of negative influences cannot be gained from the sidelines. They must be met, experienced, fought and repelled before such understanding comes. These influences can take many forms: unpleasant and lecherous monsters, in the case of John Stuart; three frightening men in the case of Bender; in our own case misfortunes and harassments of various sorts.

If the struggle with Satan were easy, the muscles of the Angels would be flabby. If the Bad were not tragic and unpleasant the paths of Heaven might be lesser trod.

The book you are about to read will be discussed by psychologists, rehashed by demonologists, burned by cowards, and alternately be used as ammunition by and preached against by Preachers. I personally don't know quite what to think of it; but I know that I must publish it.

What do you think?
**Gray Barker**

# GLOSSARY

Certain New Zealand slang terms appear in this book and are translated here to their real meanings in English.

"FAIR DINKUM": Genuine. Real. Serious.

"DICKEN": Wait on. Just a minute.

"STREWTH": An abbreviation for the words, "God s Truth."

"STRIKE!": A term used by soldiers in the First World War, being in full, "Strike a light!" Also meaning, generally, an exclamation such as "Gosh!" or "Gee!"

"COBBER": This term is used only in Australia and New Zealand, and means, "Friend."

"SHE'S RIGHT!": Used ONLY in New Zealand Means "That's all right."

"CRIKEY": This is a derivative of the word, "Christ," and is sometimes spoken as "Gripes," although the latter is more peculiar to Australia.

"STOUSH": A Kiwi soldier's term for 'Flght," or "Battle."

"RIGHT-OH": Another way of saying "Allright," and used on both sides of the Tasman Sea, in Australia and New Zealand.

## CHAPTER ONE
## THE BEGINNING

I began an active study of the UFO Enigma in 1948 and, over the first few months, dealt only with the few reports avail- able. They came mainly from America, with one or two from Australia.

My first belief was that these strange objects were interplanetary space vehicles. At that time one could suggest little else -- for the idea that Antarctica was involved did not occur to anyone connected with the investigation. In fact, it was not until 1953 that such an idea was born in my own mind.

Once I accepted it as fact, the "uncanny" began with shocking results for my co-worker and myself. It was during 1950 that I decided to form my own society; this was planned to bring together those New Zealanders interested in this new mystery, and to attempt what appeared to be the impossible: find the answer as to what the UFOs were, and from where they originated. I also wished to know why they were coming to Earth's skies, and why they had not landed to make known their intentions.

I made a note at that time, referring to the fact that the UFOs might be interested in man's devilish new toy, the Atom Bomb, and its effect on Earth-dwellers. I also noted, "Interest in man may be clinical? Why?"

This note, I see today, was filled with tremendous questions, each of which concluded with one word: "WHY?" It was a challenge, and I accepted it. I was determined to pit my own wits against those of people (?) who controlled these discs. But what could a mere 28-year-old Kiwi do to learn this secret? There was only one way. I would have to use my own common sense and work on a process of elimination. And then I had to decide how one began to investigate a mystery such as this.

The only evidence we had was the fact that a few "strange disc shaped craft were sighted over (say) Washington." Why? What had they hoped to find? What were they searching for? What made them "tick"? Who owned them?

Of questions I had an enormous number, but the facts were not yet at hand. I was determined to search out those facts. It was a challenge to a young New Zealander. I accepted it, and planned the formation of my own society, but the results of a war wound, a legacy of El Alamein, stopped my ideas for some time.

In 1952 I contacted Harold H. Fulton, who had founded Civilian Saucer Investigation, of Auckland, New Zealand, and kept him up to date on reports from my own city and immediate area. Later, through wide correspondence, I received reports from all over the world, and also passed this along to Fulton.

At first it was a most amicable association, but later it developed into something far removed from a friendship. I was urged on in my dedicated quest for information, and in my quiet research I contacted as many fellow researchers as I could in other countries, offering whatever assistance I could give. Many such researchers did not accept my offers to help, but those who did remained with me -- the most of them almost to the end. One of them stuck with me even through that.

The Hamilton, N. Z. Flying Saucer Investigation Society was formed in April 1953, and I was appointed Secretary. At the initial meeting I told those present of the five UFOs I had sighted in the preceding seven years, the first being in November, 1946, the second in 1947, the third in the same year. The next was on Easter, 1953; and two nights later I experienced another sighting, that one witnessed by my wife.

My association with the Hamilton organization lasted only about six months, after which I was expelled in "disgrace." I had worked out a theory about UFOs and had inadvertently used a copy of the Society's letterhead. The Committee objected to this, and I was expelled from their very august gathering, being allowed no chance to defend my action, since I was not informed of the meeting.

As a result of this expulsion by H.F.S.I.S., I suggested to a young lady friend that we immediately form our own organization to attack the mystery along the lines of the theory I had developed. She enthusiastically agreed, and it was from this suggestion that Flying Saucer Investigators (the formal name of our organization) was born.

We carried on this research until December 1954, when we were forced to close down after very frightening attacks from an unknown source. In that month, Barbara fled in terror, and I went to Auckland to recover my normal health with my old mother. My trip to Auckland was much different from the evil-minded suggestions that I had "gone away with that girl"!

Two and a half years later I returned to my home with the intentions of carrying out further research, but again I closed the organization, thinking of the real theory I had regarding the UFOs. Also, I remembered the dissolute and nefarious things which were said when I escorted Barbara to the cinema, or when we strolled in the moonlight, talking of our views and findings about UFOs. These cinema visits and walks were quite innocent, but the depraved minds of those who secretly watched saw only the suggestion of sensuality, the only thing their insidious minds were capable of seeing.

And so, while these evil minds concocted filthy thoughts of Barbara and me, we carried on in our attempts to solve the mystery, our time being fully taken up with our task. It is admitted that we did find time to "act the goat," and at these times I have kissed my co-worker, a fact which was pointed out to me by one of the busy-bodies. I wonder still wherein lies the sin of kissing a girl in friendship or in jest!

## CHAPTER TWO
## MY FIRST WARNING

During my research I encountered many experiences which I could only construe as being frightening, or, at the least, strange. It is difficult for me to determine if all of these experiences were connected with my UFO research, or to determine which were and which weren't. The first such experience, which I now relate, probably should be listed under the "weren't" heading, but it is definitely a part of my narrative. The date escapes me, but it happened in 1951 or 1952, as I was standing in the lounge doorway, smoking a cigarette.

The house was quiet, and I was thinking of ordinary matters, as I faced the front door, about five feet away. Suddenly I heard footsteps on the concrete path outside, and I wondered who might be calling at such a late hour. The doorbell rang and I stepped forward to greet my visitor.

No more than two or three seconds passed from the time the bell rang until I had the door open, and I was surprised and puzzled to find nobody there! I ran outside, hoping to catch the prankster. I searched the grounds without result. I was indeed puzzled, for whoever had rung my doorbell would not have had time to escape without my observing or hearing them running away. I wondered if there were indeed such things as ghosts, though I found the thought amusing and chuckled. Later, when I informed Barbara of the incident, she immediately suggested it might have involved something of supernatural nature. I laughed at her and told her I thought those things were just so much rot. Later, though, I remembered those words!

The doorbell incident first returned to mind some time in 1952, at about 11:30 P.M. I was in bed, reading, when my telephone rang. I was a trifle annoyed as I picked up the phone to answer such a late call, then even more annoyed as the following conversation took place:

"Are you John Stuart?"

"That is correct."

"You are the John Stuart who is interested in what earth men call flying saucers?"

"That's right. What can I do for you?"

"I warn you to stop interfering in affairs which do not concern you!"

"Who the hell are you talking to, mate? And who the flaming hell are you!"

"I am ???????????? from another planet." (The name I cannot remember because it seemed to be unpronounceable)

"Go to hell!" (Again I was warned, the voice adding the dangers I would face if I failed to take heed)

"Beware, Earthman!"

"You and who else, mate?" (This will serve as my answer, for the actual words I used I would not want to appear in this book)

"You have been warned!"

The line suddenly went dead. As I slowly replaced the receiver, my mind was alert to the words I had just heard. My first reaction was to treat it as a hoax, but when I sat down with a pot of beer I began to wonder.

The voice had been most strange. In quality, it was like a machine talking to me —— expressionless, cold. But that cold tone only added to its meaning. I shuddered and drank my beer. The warning had been given. Why? What did I know that was so important to this person, or thing? What did I know which was more revealing than, say, what Fulton had learned?

I lit a cigarette and told myself that some half-baked drongo had been playing games with me. I nodded. That was the answer. The world was full of these simple-minded people who had nothing better to do than play games which even a child would scorn.

## CHAPTER THREE
## SAUCERS AN "INSIDE JOB"?

Reflecting further on the telephone call, I was forced to consider the possibility that it MIGHT have been genuine. What then? But whether it had been a hoax or the real thing, I knew that I must ignore the threat. I had fought in a war for my freedom, and I wasn't going to be pushed around! Why, I mentally demanded, should some unknown person or thing tell me what to do? Again I told them to "go to hell and do your worst" in my thoughts. Later I was to believe the owner of the voice had heard those thoughts – for "they" did do their "worst!"

In spite of this warning, I continued my investigations, arriving at no concrete conclusions. These theories I evolved seemed too fantastic for reality, so I delved into other mysteries, including Spiritualism. As I read books on this subject, I wondered. Was there any connection between the dead and the UFO mystery? The idea seemed stupid – but was it? Hadn't I been a regular attendant at my Church of England before leaving home to follow life's rough path? There was this character, the "Devil." was it too fantastic to believe that Satan was behind the discs? That they were a sign of his own activity? No, that was too damndably fantastic! And this was getting a little close to Black Magic.

I abandoned the idea. If it were fantastic, then what were these discs? There seemed to be something supernatural about them; Or did they really travel over the vast distances, through the void of space to observe the earth? And if so, why? Was it because of the Atom Bombs the United States used to blast Nagasaki and Hiroshima into near oblivion? If so, still WHY? Why didn't discs come while the ruins were still smoking? Why wait until the dead were cold and the smoke gone? I told myself it could be because of the vast distances they would have to travel through space. It couldn't be that, for if these beings had sufficient knowledge to build a craft to travel through space, wasn't it possible they could skip down here in a hurry? How? The fourth dimension? I gasped and decided this was a new possibility. It was crazy!

Satan. Black Magic. Two Japanese cities blasted to end in a cruel war. The fourth dimension. These things raced through my mind. I read all the books I could locate on Black Magic, and decided it was too evil. Evil? There had to be some connection with Satan! But what? And why? This troubled me. There had to be an answer! But what was the answer? I didn't know.

Alright, I remarked mentally, say these discs do come from another planet. Which planet was the most suspect? I began to feel like a detective. One of a detective's jobs is to first determine and examine suspects. And my strongest feeling as to suspects involved the closest planet – MARS. Allowing that the discs did come from Mars, the old question again arose: WHY???? Was it really because of the atom blasts? Surely the flash wasn't bright enough to be seen across all those miles. It would seem illogical that the blast or radiation effect could be detected that far away. If the closest planet might be ruled out, then what?

A good detective's job is made somewhat easier if he can be cognizant of an "inside job." Although I didn't consider myself a good detective, this thought did come to mind.

What if the discs came from somewhere CLOSER? The moon? Still unlikely. But wait, what might be closer than that? The Earth? I laughed aloud at my thoughts.

This was, indeed, impossible. Before long, I told myself, I would be seeing little green men, and then the health authorities would come and toss me into a padded cell! Again I looked at Mars and wondered. WHAT THE BLAZES WERE THESE THINGS?

I figuratively lived with the discs, and even slept with them on my mind, and constantly watched the sky. I saw them, alright, and for my efforts heard the infantile laughing of the childish scoffers.

# CHAPTER FOUR
## THE THING IN THE DESERT

But there was one sighting I had forgotten about. What was the thing I had seen in the Western Desert? It was November, 1941. My battalion lay in the dark, waiting for the signal which would send us forward to see and face death. A place called Sidi Rezegh. In front of us was the dark outline of the escarpment, and on top was the block-house. Nerves tensed. Safety catches were released. On our rifles, the bayonets, 17 inches of the best British steel, gave confidence. I wiped the dust from my eyes, turning my head away from the wireless at my side. I STARED BLANKLY. WHAT . . . ?

Behind us, and about five or six feet above the sand was an orange ball. It made no movement. I wiped the sweat from my brow, and decided it was a secret weapon of the enemy. I had no time to think any more of it. The signal came, and what remained of my battered unit went into that cruel and shocking carnage. I forgot the strange ball when I saw men fall in death, when I heard the cries of the wounded and the terrible sounds of the battle around me.

What had the orange ball been? Where had it come from? What had it been doing there. Why had it apparently been interested in we Earthmen, waiting to fight in that game of death? The Allies wouldn't claim it, and the Germans were indignant when asked if they owned it.

"Strewth, no!" declared the Kiwis.

"Nein!" cried the Germans.

So nobody owned this thing. And who would own a huge ball-like object which hung in mid-air, its glow like that of a huge furnace. And how did it suddenly extinguish its glow and race away to the south? Where did it go? I had no ideas to put forward.

The entire mystery was frightening in its immensity, so I returned to a study of space travel, deciding this might be the best vantage point from which to attack the Enigma. I was to spend many long hours with such questions as "Why?" "Where?" and "Which?" It was most discouraging, but I gained heart and pressed on ... a fatal mistake in view of what occurred later.

It seemed there were saucers everywhere. Again the question: "what are these things?" They had been recorded in the earliest historical writings, and while there was the possibility that some of the ancient reports could have referred to heavenly bodies, some of them, quite obviously, described the very same type of UFOs we were seeing in the Twentieth Century.

The earliest report of UFOs over New Zealand was made in 1910, when a cigar-shaped object was sighted. The scoffers, no doubt, insisted it was the planet Venus, a weather balloon (if they had them at that time), or other natural objects or phenomena. But the fact remains that at 11:00 on that evening in January, 1910, a number of people in the town of Invercargill (situated at the southern end of the South Island of New Zealand) did see a cigar-shaped object at a (approximate) height of 100 feet. They also observed a door in the side of the huge object open, and a figure appear, which called out in a foreign tongue. The figure then moved back inside, the door closed, and the object sped away.

Now it is necessary to explain to the doubtful that those who saw the craft had just emerged from a local pub (the public bar where, in those old days, beer was served only until 11:00 P.M.) after a few pots of brew. The scoffer will now nod wisely, thinking he has the perfect answer: they were "shicker"! Ah , but we must spoil this theory! It is recorded that the Vicar, Policeman, the town's Mayor, and other people of good character and importance, also saw the object, and it is unlikely that of these particular people would have been having "a Spot."' So what was it? I don't know. But I an certain of two things it was not: It certainly was not Venus, nor was it a weather balloon!

# CHAPTER FIVE
# MAPPING THE SAUCERS

I have gone into the matter of my short tenure as an officer in the Hamilton Flying Saucer Investigation Society. When I was expelled from that organization I asked Barbara Turner to assist me in forming what was to be known as Flying Saucer Investigators. She agreed to help me. Knowing the problems of a group of individuals, with many conflicting ideas, we decided to limit the organization to only two people, Barbara and myself.

Flying Saucer Investigators vowed to tell the truth, to make known to others our views and findings, and to assist in bringing about the final solution to the Enigma. We didn't bargain for the fiendish humans about us who found a reprehensible delight in blackening our association. Soon we met frigid and frosty looks. We were shunned. And these malicious humans (?) delved into their stygian minds to find the vicious venom to throw at us. But we laughed at their pitiful efforts, often quoting an old Chinese proverb, "He who paddles in a stagnant pool will find only mud." Maybe these evil ones found that in their own minds. And in spite of this insidious talk, Barbara and I were able to effectively pursue our research.

We made contact with a U. S. researcher, Gray Barker, who became a firm friend, and assisted us in many ways, keeping us informed about the American scene as it was affected by the UFOs. He was, and still is, a dinkum cobber. Later, he showed his friendship by selecting us as two of the very few to whom a copy of a startling report was sent. We were grateful for this, and guarded the report to keep it secret as we had been requested to do I refer here to the report on (using the name later coined by Gray in his book) Gordon Smallwood. This is not the real name of this researcher, but it will hide the real identity.

With the formation of FSI, Barbara and I would meet each evening to discuss the latest reports, and to talk at length on some new idea we had thought of during the day. Quite often our meetings lasted until 3:00 A.M., and this gave fresh fuel to the evil minded who slandered us. But these meetings were filled with great interest, and the time soon passed, leaving us with so little said and so much to say. During those early days of FSI I related to Barbara the sightings I had made, the strange experiences, and the views I had taken on UFOs. I made these reports to her as detailed as possible, so that she might have a clearer picture or the case, and as the evenings passed she became a very good pupil, and began to advance her own ideas. They were worth listening to. She made many sound suggestions, among which was a plan to draw a huge map of the world on which would be placed all the sightings we had in our possession.

"After we have all the sightings in place, Johnnie," she explained, "we hook them all up with lines to show the direction of travel. You know, the direction these things cane from, and the direction in which they returned. To and from, Johnnie, is the idea."

"whaffor?" I asked.

"By doing this," she told me, "we will have some indication as to where these things come from."

I looked at her in startled amazement. "I once thought it was possible that these things came from the Earth, but dropped it as fantastic. Now you have suggested it tool Why?" I asked her.

She lit a cigarette rather thoughtfully, looking at my collection of books. "It's obvious, isn't it?" she murmured, looking up at me.

"Obvious? What is?" I inquired, puzzled.

She sat down, and then said, "I'll explain when I draw our map. Now, do you have a huge sheet of paper?"

I located what she required and sat watching as her slim fingers guided a pencil to form the shapes of countries of the earth. It was a long job, and it was not until the following evening that we were able to look upon it as completed. As Barbara lightly tapped her teeth with her pencil, I asked, "Now, what's the next move? To mark in all the sightings?"

"Yes, Johnnie." She soon completed this section and there were the lines between each sighting. "Now, let's look at it from this angle. These saucers have to have a base, don't they? And what would be better than some vast, uninhabited part of the earth?"

"Agreed. But where?"

She returned to the map and lightly traced along the lines with her finger, a puzzled frown on her brow. "I'm not certain yet, Johnnie." Again she marked in some lines, and her hand stopped, her pencil poised like some slim pointer. "It...it can't be!" she whispered loudly.

"What can't be, Barbara?"

"How about an area of ice, John?" she asked in a quiet voice.

I stepped to her side, close to the map, and stared at it, my eyes following the maze of lines. It was a little confusing, or I was tired, for the lines merely showed a tangle. Barbara slipped her hands into the pocket of her slacks, as a slight pale- ness showed beneath her make-up. "That's it, John," she said soberly.

Again I stared at the map, and with a gasp, saw what she meant. The lines had converged on Antarctica! I saw immediately the enormity of our discovery, and was all for contacting other researchers immediately.

"Wouldn't it be better to wait, Johnnie, until we have something concrete to tell them?" Barbara asked.

"I know we could write to Gray and tell him, for instance, that we have a six foot long map of the world on which we've drawn a maze of lines. We could say these lines converge on Antarctica. But what would that mean? Just that we have a lot of lines on a map which converge on the South Pole region."

She shook her head. "No, I'm all for waiting until we really have something dinkum to offer. Think so, boy?"

Reluctantly I agreed. And this information was destined to be hidden for a long time. But that evening I agreed to wait, and we set about examining the possibility that the UFOs were based on Antarctica, asking Barbara just where she found this idea, for I had the impression she had thought in that direction before she made the map, and that it had been the final thing which had convinced her.

"From a number of things, John. One from you when you told me of the Shaver business. Another when it was quite obvious that the saucers seemed to come from and travel to the south. It added up. Like adding one and one making two." She accepted the cigarette I offered her, and then said, "Shall we study it further?"

"Too right, Barbs. I'm all for it," I replied eagerly. "And the first question to answer once we decide the saucers come from the pole is this: WHY?"

Barbara nodded. "Yes, John. why? Why are they using the earth as a base? Why don't they land where they can be studied? What are they scared of? What sort of people, if they are people like us, control them? Are the saucers we see manned? Are they robots? What are they made of? What makes 'em go?" She grinned. "There sure is a lot to learn."

"That, my dear, is the understatement of the century!"

She laughed softly. "Alright, mate, where does one start? Say something silly and trust it turns out right?"

I grinned at her, and said, "Something silly, is it? Lemme see, Barbs." I thought. "Got it. One day, a long time of people lived at the pole, and there came upon them a terrible catastrophe in which they were frozen stiff. They were in a state of suspended animation. Thousands of years later, in a terrible war, an equally terrible bomb was exploded and the heat from it melted the ice to thaw the lost race. And along came the day when these people tried out the ships which were locked in the ice from the day when the big freeze came." I grinned. "And they live happily ever after," I laughed.

"You silly idiot, Johnnie!" giggled Barbara. "Of all the silly ideas! Deep frozen people," she grinned. "And deep frozen flying saucers!"

"Well," I remarked in mock dismay, "you did ask me to say something silly. And I did just that."

"I know. Now let's be serious. Shall we?" Her eyes twinkled. "About saucers, I mean too, you idiot."

"Alright. I'll be serious," I chuckled. "It's almost 1954, and as soon as the New Year comes, I'll be serious for a whole year. Howzat?"

"Bet you can't."

"On. It's a bet, Barbs!" I grinned at her. Had we known what the year of 1954 had in store for us, I venture to suggest that we would have forgotten not only our bet, but every- thing to do with UFOs! It was to be a year of terror. Of horror and fear.

## CHAPTER SIX
## ANCIENT PEOPLES AND THE UFO

New Year's day, 1954, was behind us, and we commenced a serious study of the Antarctica theory. As we did so we began to see the terrible possibilities of this idea. Could it be that the saucers were literally on New Zealand's own doorstep? And if so, what was their purpose in being there? How did they manage to survive the intense cold?

I mentioned to Barbara the possibility that Admiral Byrd had seen something of the UFOs when he had been on his polar expeditions.

"Yes, he must have seen something strange down there, John. It has been rumored, hasn't it, that he was officially silenced before he could tell WHAT, though? Pity, really."

I formed new ideas as we talked of Antarctica. "I believe the polar region to be mountainous, and it is quite likely that there are plenty of places where a UFO, or a number of them, could hide away from the eyes of even the most careful expeditions. It's a big thing to study, isn't it?"

Barbara settled back in her chair, frowning a little as she toyed with her cigarette. "But why do the UFOs want to hang around at the pole, Johnnie?"

"Wish I knew. If I could answer that, Barbs, I could answer the entire case. Couldn't I?" I paused and lit up a fresh cigarette. "Of course it could have something to do with the ice cap. It's diminishing in size, isn't it?"

"Yes," nodded Barbara. "And that could be part of the answer, couldn't it? These saucer people, if we can call them that, know the manner in which the pole is melting and have come here to study the effects. A cold idea, but possible. Anyway, if our ice cap was to melt that much, then heaven help us! It would cause our planet to topple, wouldn't it? It wouldn't take much to make it topple either, flinging us into oblivion." Then she added quietly, "Not a pleasant thought, is it?"

"No," I replied, "it's a nasty thought. Anyway, keep talking, you might come up with something really startling."

(Editor's note: We believe John and Barbara were in error about the melting. To our knowledge, there is some indication that the North Pole is melting slightly, and that ice is building up at the South Pole. The latter condition, so states engineer Hugh A. Brown, could lead to a toppling and change of axis of the earth. - G.B.)

She nodded and then grinned happily. "Keep talking, the boy says! Gee, just think what our nasty minded friends are now saying about our being here together. And we are just talking as we should be. What a letdown for them, eh? Where was I? Oh, yes. This idea of the earth toppling might not be so silly, you know, after reading Velikovsky's book. He related there how some cosmic upheaval affected the earth all those thousands of years ago, and how that mammoth was found in Siberia with grass still in its mouth."

She paused for a moment and then continued. "Of course may have nothing to do with the Antarctica idea, but it's in the same category, isn't it? Anyway, whatever happened to that mammoth was so sudden that it was deep-frozen in a split second of time.

She snapped her fingers expressively. "Bang! Just like that! Quick. Fast. Too fast to understand what had turned you into an iceberg." She was now smiling eagerly as she snapped her lighter, drawing smoke into her lungs.

"Now, allowing that the earth is in a similar danger, is it so silly to believe the saucer people are coming here to see just what is happening to us? That the UFOs are really space vehicles used by Martian scientists?" she asked

"Yes, it's possible," I agreed. "But seriously, why would they come all that way just to see us meet our doom?"

"Because, maybe, they were once earth dwellers," Barbara answered calmly.

Barbara said this so seriously and so knowingly that I started. Not that the idea was so blasted startling, but it must have been the way she said it. It was almost as if someone other than Barbara were talking. I believe that was the moment that I, in looking back, first noticed some change taking place in Barbara, a change that was indicative of untold suffering she, directly, and I, indirectly, would undergo. I wish our association had been cut off at that time, but what is done cannot be undone.

I remember that I commented enthusiastically: "They....hey, dicken! That's too flaming fantastic, Barbs!"

"It is?" she inquired, a trifle archly.

"Fair dinkum, kid, you're just being funny," I told her with a grin.

Barbara raised her eyebrows, and asked me with mock aloofness, "Am 1? well, you like to study old ruins, don't you?"

"Old buildings? Yes, I like to study them. Why?"

"Well, do you know where the Aztecs went?"

"The Aztecs? Why they just up and......" I stopped. Where the devil DID they go? I poured a glass of beer, chuckled and said, "To be honest, Barbara, I forgot to ask the last one I saw."

Barbara frowned at me. "Oh! Do be a little serious."

"You're right, Barb. Alright, I just dunno what happened to them?"

"You see? Now listen to me, Johnnie. The Aztecs were a race of very clever people, and erected fine temples which the modern builder would have quite a time with. They made a deep study of science, and the scientific side of life, seeing that the earth was doomed to destruction, or at the least, its living beings were in danger of destruction. They could foresee this terrible catastrophe, and immediately went about leaving the earth to escape death; and after they departed, this deathly cold struck, deep- freezing any living creatures remaining. And it was swift, too."

"Then you believe the Aztecs lived here on earth as a civilized race when the mighty mammoth roamed the earth?"

"Exactly."

"And providing this theory of yours is correct, what happened to those who couldn't escape?"

She shrugged her shoulders. "I have no idea, really. Bit by bit we can look into that."

"Where's the proof that all this happened?"

"None, old thing. But there are those temples in a verdant jungle. So where did the blokes and their sheilas go? They just couldn't say, Oh, blow this, mate! Let's go look for another world!'" She chuckled.

"You silly idiot," I laughed.

She grinned, and then said, "Let's be serious, eh? They must have gone somewhere. And there's the statues on Easter Island What happened to those who quarried the stone and cut the blocks to shape? Something caused them to down tools in a flaming hurry and bolt like blue blazes. Where to? Why? What caused them to leave? Was there something to fear here on this planet?"

"Granting they left as you say, why should their descendants want to return to study our mode of living?"

"As I said before, Johnnie, the earth may be approaching some sort of catastrophe, and they are clinically interested in the means of our escape. To them, we earth people are just guinea pigs in a matter of life and death."

"A very cold thought," I remarked grimly.

"We have to be coldly analytical in such investigations, and all our research, John."

"I grant that, Barbara. But all this must have happened countless thousands of years ago! And that being so, where did you, me, the other people of this earth come from? I mean the inhabitants who escaped were alright, but what of those who didn't escape? Naturally, they died in the catastrophe, and so there was no life left. There were no white men, no Indians, no Chinese, or anyone else. Where did we all come from if there was no life remaining to reproduce?"

"To answer that, Johnnie, we must go back to the Bible, to the time of Adam and Eve."

"Why them, Barbara?"

"Because, Johnnie, they were the first to arrive after the terror. I believe that Adam and Eve were two people who lived on another planet. Their home was a place where there was no sin, no crime, and where everyone lived a perfect existence. The Bible tells us that Eve picked a forbidden apple, and to bring that crime up to date, let's say that she committed some crime against the society in which she lived. They were punished, and to be sure they didn't commit any further crimes on their own planet, they were exiled to earth, naked and alone. They were the first to return after the catastrophe, and soon set about making a home on a strange planet.

"Of course, I refuse to believe they were the mother and father of the earth people who today inhabit this planet, but they did have children, and one of them returned to the other planet to find himself a mate. It's obvious that all these stories have some basis in fact, one must look closer to find what might really have happened. To find the truth is rather simple, or at least I should say, I think it is simple. All you have to do is study the old story and bring it up to date."

"Go on," I urged, fascinated not only by her remarks, but rather puzzled by her erudition. These long discourses were unlike my friend. It seemed as though "something had come over her," so to speak.

"It could have happened just as I say. Ancient history is full of such creation stories."

"But what have UFOs to do with Adam and Eve?"

"How do you think our naked couple got here? They could hardly have walked, could they?" she grinned.

"Hardly! So you believe they came by disc?"

"Yes, and to get here, maybe they used the moon as some sort of stepping stone."

"And what do you think about the beings who use the UFOs now?" I asked her.

Barbara looked thoughtful, and admitted, "I don't know." "Of course," she then added, "there may be two groups of them at work. One bunch the goody—goods, and B the baddies. The good space people wants us to live a decent life in spite of their clinical interest in us, while the bad ones are out to make us live a lecherous life."

"That's something of what Shaver said," I advised her.

"And so I have said it."

"But what has all this to do with the ice cap down below on our back doorstep?" I inquired.

"Nothing. I just think up these ideas on the hope it will give us a new lead, that's all," she murmured.

"Well, forget your 'goodie' and 'baddie' space people idea. Your first thought was more interesting."

Barbara smiled. "Yes, I like it too. At the same time, Johnnie, we should look at this idea of bad and good, or good and evil, whichever sounds right."

"I've tried that one."

"What, Johnnie?"

"Good and evil, of course," I explained.

She grinned at me. "I know. You said you'd had a pretty wild time at the war."

I laughed at her audacious grin. "I was talking about UFO research! Not that kind of evil, you idiot!"

"Right-o, mate. But I still think it's worth thinking about." She looked at her watch. "Strewth! It's almost half past one! I'm away on a fast camel! More talk tomorrow night, Johnnie. Goodnight, mate," she smiled.

## CHAPTER SEVEN
## R.A.F. REPORTS OBJECT

When we met the next evening, Barbara seemed to be more of her "old self" again. I mention this partly in light of what you will read later and partly in defense of Barbara.

Barbara had impressed me as a sweet, kind, innocent girl — that was the reason I could work with her, even late of nights, without feeling guilty of anything that the rumor-mongers no doubt spread.

There are, indeed, such things as love, and physical desire. But transcending the latter, and maybe even love, is another feeling, that of deep friendship of pure nature. That is how I felt about her.

We studied reports of "little green men" allegedly seen in remote parts of the United States. Barbara asked me what I thought about them.

"Just a lot of rot," I growled.

"Oh, I don't know, Johnnie," she remonstrated; "There may be some truth in the reports!"

"Why," I frowned.

"well, look at this one," and she held out a clipping. "It says here that a chap saw one of the little men near his mine. The small bloke wanted some water, it seems."

I lit a cigarette and said, grumpily, "So did the bloke who claimed he saw the little character! Only he wanted some water for his flaming whisky!"

"Don't be so nasty, Johnnie!" admonished Barbara. "Lots of people see things which are never explained! And never believed either!"

"I know that, my dear," I replied, and then told her again of the strange thing I saw at Sidi Rezegh in 1941.

"And did the other soldiers see it too?"

"Never heard if they did," I answered. "After the stoush was over, we who were left talked about the fighting, and of those who hadn't made it. At that time the silly thing in the sky just didn't seem to be important. Certainly, someone else must have seen it. But out of my battalion more than a third were killed or wounded. If others did see it, my guess is that they, like I, didn't think it was important enough to talk about at that time."

"Strange, alright," remarked Barbara. "It makes think, doesn't it, of that report in the British newspaper of the object which the authorities said was a weather balloon."

The report had been published in THE DAILY MIRROR, dated November 19, 1953.  Banner headlines shouted:

MYSTERY "SPOT" SEEN ON LONDON RADAR SCREEN TWO R.A.F. PILOTS REPORT "OBJECT".

Radar screens of twice recently picked up mysterious objects in the sky. The most recent was on Tuesday, when Sergeant-Major Ernest Stead, a radar instructor, was making a routine check at the headquarters of the 265 Regiment Heavy A.F., at Lee Green, Lewisham.

With four civilian helpers, he got on the screen very strong target" at a height of about 60,000 feet.  The object was moving slowly, and it gradually went out of range.

Sergeant-Major Stead reported the incident to his adjutant, Captain Fowler, who told Brigade headquarters. Captain Fowler said last night, "It is impossible to say what the object was. Because of the fog, it could not be seen through the sighting telescope, but the strength of the signal seemed to indicate that the object was of colossal size."

The report continued with details of a sighting made by Sergeant Waller, on November 3, 1953, about the same time of the day. In his report to Captain Fowler, Sergeant Waller said "We got a very strong target between 2:30 and 3:1 .P.M. The signal was extremely strong. I estimated the object's height at 61,000 feet. It was stationary for some time, then moved slowly away and gradually went out of range. It disappeared at about 43,000 feet. As soon as I lost it from the screen I went out to see if I could see it. Through the sighting telescope, I saw a round or spherical object, a brilliant white in color, still stationary. Although it looked small through the telescope, it must have been of great size to be visible at that height."

Two R.A.F. pilots stationed at West Malling, Kent not identify but about four Two R.A.F. pilots stationed at Kent, saw an object that they could identify on the same day as Sergeant Waller, but about four hours earlier the following day it seemed the authorities were making an all-out effort to ridicule this latest sighting. One headline read:

"IT MIGHT HAVE BEEN A BALLOON."

And on Page 2 there appeared a large headline:

"FLYING SAUCER WAS A BIG BALLOON."

The "flying saucer" reported by army radar men on November 3 was a balloon, the Air Ministry said last night

It was said to have been sent up by meteorological men from an Air Ministry weather station at Crawley, Sussex. Said an Air Ministry spokesman: "It has been established that there was a balloon up at that time and in that area, and there can be little doubt that this was the object sighted."

The object reported and tracked by the radar men was also reported by the crew of a Vampire jet fighter. But the man who tracked the "saucer"....was unconvinced: "I would have never have been able to see a balloon 12 miles away if it had been only 12 feet across, as the Ministry says it was. Suppose it was a balloon we saw, what was it the R.A.F. saw? They reported it at 10:20 A.M., but according to the Ministry that balloon did not go up until 2:00 P.M."

After we had read this report, Barbara remarked that it was strange how the Air Ministry had avoided any mention of the object reported on November 19. I pointed some half-hearted attempt to ridicule this too and read her a small item: "IT MIGHT HAVE BEEN A BALLOON. A possible explanation for the 'mystery spot' on the radar screen was given by the Air Ministry last night. A spokesman said it could have been a weather balloon."

There were a couple of other lines saying that the balloons carry a metal tail which is designed to give the balloons a strong "echo."

It was interesting to note that in this case, as in contrast to the previous one, the Ministry said it was a "possible explanation." Nothing definite about it. Just "possible."

"The authorities have spoken!" mocked Barbara. "There we have the solution to the UFOs! You and I, Johnnie, are just wasting our time, as are so many other researchers throughout the world. We should have more common sense than to mistake the UFO for a common weather balloon! And to think that over the last couple of hundred years there have been weather balloons drifting about the sky! And in a lot of cases the said balloons even had the audacity to go against the wind! Anyway, I always understood weather balloons were something new. Something that our ancient forefathers didn't know anything about! But, there you are, Johnnie, the UFOs are just weather balloons, and not even the pilots of the fighter planes know any better!" she added in deep scorn.

Those pilots who see these so-called balloons will have to be better trained," I said. "To think that it's youngsters like them who will defend the Commonwealth in the event of another war! Maybe we should let the authorities pilot the planes? They know what's a weather balloon and what's something else!"

"Yes," nodded Barbara. "And just how long will these jack-booted officials go on with their stupidity? Why won't they admit the truth?"

"Maybe they don't know any better, Barbara."

"And they are allowed to make such childish statements?"

"But they have no real answer to the mystery. And to hide their ignorance, these so-called learned men jump to their feet and wave their arms in the air as they make their idiotic press releases! They're too afraid to admit they have no idea of what the UFOs are!"

Barbara smiled at my harsh tone, and said, "But when that object was sighted from the Dak, the local authorities must have decided to ignore it, eh? There was one which no one has explained. Of course," she said, with a taunting smile, "it was just a weather balloon, wasn't it, Johnnie?"

The report appeared in the EVENING POST of January 11, 1952, and read:

## AIR-TO-AIR SIGHTING OF UNKNOWN OBJECT NEAR KUITI

The first recorded air-to-air sighting of an unknown object in New Zealand occurred at 9:27 last night. The copilot of a National Airways Corporation DC-3, First Officer K. G. Bond, watched a brilliant reddish-orange light move steadily across the path of the liner. He thinks it was too low and traveling too slowly to have been a meteor.

The Dakota at the time was on its way from Wellington to Auckland, and 15 miles west of Kuiti.
First Officer Bond at once checked by radio with Air Traffic Control in Wellington and was told that no aircraft were flying in the Wellington or Auckland control areas.

When he was startled by the light dead ahead, First Officer Bond had just looked up from checking his instruments in the cockpit.

"It was brighter than any meteor and was moving from west to east in a straight line," he said today. "It was about the size of Venus in the sky and had a definite tail of color. Meteors usually travel in a curved path and speed up. They go much faster than this light traveled. It seemed to be about one and a half miles in front and at 8,000 feet -- 1,000 feet higher than the aircraft. But it must have been farther away as the light would have moved towards the star- board wingtip in the 45 seconds I watched it."

The Captain was called to the cockpit, but the light had then disappeared.

"It was fairly cloudy below, but was clearer towards Tauranga and Rotorua," added First Officer Bond. "I hope somebody over there saw it. I always regarded reports of 'flying saucers' with skepticism. I am not prepared to say this was a 'flying saucer,' but I am convinced now there is something in the reports."

I remarked to Barbara, "And there is another case where a reliable pilot has seen one of these things while in flight. I suppose one could safely say that it was not a balloon? That the stock reply is a little out of the line of sanity in this report?"

"Maybe K. G. wasn't feeling well, and was just seeing things, Johnnie," she grinned. "Isn't that another stock answer? That we who do see these UFOs are just seeing things?"

"There are lots of excuses and explanations," I answered.

"Maybe, of course, he saw a weather balloon? Or was it the planet Venus? Amazing, y'know, the antics that these weather balloons and poor old Venus get up to! Of course, Johnnie, like our cobber, K. G. Bond, we're just plain silly! The very idea of you and I actually believing in flying saucers!" she said in a mocking tone.

She stared at her cigarette for a moment, and then went on, still derisively: "We must be silly, y'know, to mistake a UFO for a common weather balloon. Can't understand how we could be so flaming stupid, can you? Why even that cigar thing we saw last week was only the planet Venus in disguise!"

"If the pilot was tired and seeing things, why wasn't he grounded? Why allow him to fly a liner and risk his passengers' lives?"

"For the very same reason as were other pilots left to fly after sighting a UFO," Barbara told me aggressively. "The authorities wouldn't be game to ground these men, so they allow them to fly, knowing full well there is something more there than they care to admit. If, and I say if, these things are just weather balloons, how is it that the said thing can travel against the wind? How is it that a balloon can travel at great speeds? Stop and start? Reverse its direction of flight? Of course," she cried in a contemptuous tone, "there might be one of those official types inside it, eh?" She laughed. "And in both cases, there would be a lot of hot air!"

"You're becoming a fair dinkum researcher, aren't you," I chuckled.

## CHAPTER EIGHT
## BARBARA'S STRANGE ACTIONS

"Well," replied Barbara, warmly, "I do have some brains, Johnnie! Anyway, let's forget these idiots." She was silent for a moment, and then asked, "Johnnie, what is down at Antarctica? Ice, I realize. But what I mean is this: What did Admiral Byrd see? Was it the UFOs in their true plane?"

"Yes," I murmured, "What did he see?" It was a most interesting question, I realized, as I looked toward my companion.

She sat in her chair, relaxed, with a deep, thoughtful expression in her eyes. I momentarily forgot the UFOs, and allowsed my thoughts to dwell on this attractive young woman. Young, attractive looks, a slim figure, a deep sense of humor, and rather clownish when she was happy, and that was most of the time. She was lost in thought as I stared at her. Her lips were slightly parted in a sort of eagerness, and I wondered just what was going on in her mind. Was she thinking of some new idea that affected the research we were doing? Or was she thinking of other things?

As far as I knew, she had no boy friends, and since she had been spending almost every evening at my home, discussing the saucers, I figured she had no interest in any boy, at least for the present.

It did seem wrong to me that she should be wasting her hours talking with someone much older than herself; she should be out with a boy, talking of her future, of love, marriage and children. I smiled inwardly. She would make someone happy eventually, and later be a young New Zealand mother.

I reflected on myself, when I had been her age. I had spent those similar years with a deadly rifle in my hands, fighting a war that was to bring peace and freedom to mankind, whatever his race or creed. I felt bitter for a moment. Where was the peace? Where was the happiness of living? Again I saw the erupting countryside, the sand of the desert stretching far into the distance, the snarling stutter of machine guns, the sharp crack of a rifle. Youth. It had gone in that hell! We went away as mere boys, and those of us who were lucky came back as old men of twenty-four and twenty-five. Youth was lost. And in its loss we had known only hell!

I looked again at Barbara. She and the boys her age were being spared all that. Despite my bitter feelings of a few moments past, I could feel glad for Barbara and them.

She looked up at me, the smile fading from her lips. "What...what's wrong, Johnnie?" she whispered, leaning forward.

"Just thinking," I replied. "Anyway, we were talking about UFOs."

She ignored my mention of the saucers, and asked, "But you said you were thinking. Of what?" she insisted.

I didn't want to talk about it, but to satisfy her, I said, "Of life. The years we lost at the war, and all that."

"But wasn't it an education...in some ways?"

"Yes, I agree. But it doesn't bring back the lost years, does it? There's thousands of us, Kiwis, Americans, Australians, English and so on. So many who wonder what it was all about." I lit a cigarette. "However, that's a man's job, and now it's over, little one."

A very strange look came over Barbara's face, one I had never noticed before. It was almost as if her features had hardened. Maybe it was the way the light caught her face as she turned slightly, but I imagined she suddenly looked much older.

"Yes, a man's job," she nodded. "Gee, I'm glad I'm a girl. We have more fun. We can make any boy we like go half-silly. I like to be kissed. And I like to tease boys." She grinned.

I was taken aback by suddenly facing an entirely new facet of her personality. I could only mumble, "What do you mean?"

"Lots of ways," she grinned again. "With a partly open shirt. Brief shorts. All that." Her smile turned more sensual.

I laughed nervously. "You're a scamp," I chided, "Even dressed as you are." A fear played on my mind, as I thought of something more to say, something that would get the subject back on our research.

Then she said something that for the first time made me fully realize that something had somehow "taken over" Barbara, that a new type of personality was somehow coming through.

"Why? Frightened of me?" she mocked.

I said nothing.

"I'd like to sit here naked. Like me to?" She whispered the latter in a very suggestive manner.

"Please, Barbara," I pleaded, trying to find some way out of the embarrassing situation.

Suddenly she herself switched the subject, but I could detect the same strange look on her face.

"Ice," she remarked. "Ice reflects light, doesn't it, Johnnie?"

It was as though her outrageous idea of undressing was suddenly gone, and had never been thought of.

"Yes, and in a mass like the southern polar cap it would act like a huge mirror."

She was silent for a moment, and then said, "I'm going to let my thoughts run wild and see what I come up with."

"Alright," I said guardedly.

"The ice reflects light just like a huge mirror, throwing light into the sky. Light, in turn, plays some funny tricks on the human eye. And it could be possible that the ice causes us to see funny things, too." She lit a cigarette and looked at me. "The UFOs are above the earth observing. Crossing their own flight paths. Minding their own business. And the ice at the south pole is reflecting an image like a mirror. I don't know sufficient about light to make this any clearer, nor to explain in technical terms what I have in mind, but I think you will see what I'm getting at. The UFOs might be anywhere above the pole and the ice captures the image, reflecting it so we can see it all."

I took up the idea. "Yes, and the fact that the UFOs are on the ice would cause your idea to work just the same. Man can bend light, and so can nature. what you are suggesting is that the UFOS are caused by a mirage. Possible, I agree."

"I think it is feasible, too, Johnnie. But first we must believe that the UFOs are either on the ice or somewhere above it. But I like to believe they are using the pole as a sort of base."

A new theory was forming in my mind, but for the moment I returned to Barbara's theory. "But, why do they insist on congregating at the pole? Why not, say, the Sahara? Or, again, the upper reaches of the Amazon?"

"The Sahara is too open, Johnnie," Barbara said. "No, I think the ice cap is the better place. You see, there may be some mineral down there that they are interested in. How do you like that?"

"Again, quite feasible. But there's a hell of a lot more to it all than that."

"H'm," nodded Barbara. "I see that," she agreed, slowly pressing the cigarette in the ashtray. "I'll think about it in bed. Now I must go, Johnnie."

I walked to the gate with her, and it seemed that once again Barbara was the same innocent young person she had been before her strange conversation of that evening.

I opened the gate and told her to sleep well. She paused momentarily, and I stood there, just a bit embarrassed by the silence. Suddenly she threw her arms around my waist, pressed her head to my shoulder, and whispered, "Help me, Johnnie, help me! Before I could ask her what was wrong she had released me and was running down the walkway.

## CHAPTER NINE
## THE PEOPLE OF THE POLES

As I lay in bed, I thought more about Barbara's strange attitude. Had her delving into the UFO secret affected her in some odd way? My first thoughts were to end the association immediately, and to do my research alone.

Then I thought of her parting remark, "Help me!" and my decision changed. Barbara was a dear friend. None but the purest thoughts had passed my mind as we had worked the evenings together. Throughout our association, a genuine affection had developed in my heart for her. If she were in the need of help, maybe it was because I had introduced her to this weird subject of saucers.

I knew Barbara could come to no harm, physically, from me. If something else were harming her, maybe I should try and do something about it. So I decided to continue the association, at least until I knew just what was wrong.

The next morning a rather strange new theory started running through my mind -- a theory which to some degree repelled me. I tried putting it from my mind, but it continued to annoy me all day. I decided not to mention this theory to Barbara, particularly because of what had passed the night before.

When we met that evening Barbara appeared quite her old self, and she began our work by again getting out the world map and going over it.

"I'm more convinced than ever that the saucers are based at the South Pole," she began, then noticing what she later described as a "blank look" on my face, she asked, with some concern, "Why, Johnnie, what's wrong?"

I said nothing, and just sat there, staring, I remember, at the ashtray, which had two or three cigarette remains in it. I felt remarkably light, though not dizzy. I knew I was not drunk, for I had not even had a glass of beer yet. I really cannot describe the sensation I felt, but the best way to put it is to say that it seemed that somebody or something was staring at me -- yet staring deep inside me.

"What's wrong? You're not acting right?" she continued.

I began speaking, as if I had very little control of what I was saying. I can remember what was happening very well, for I can recall what I said, almost word for word. Barbara continued to look at me in amazement as I spoke in what she later described as "more of a monotone" than my usual voice, which I certainly do not believe is usually monotonous:

"For a long time we've talked about Antarctica. We've decided it is from here that the UFOs come. I believe this to be correct, but not all come from there, of course. To explain, we must return to a time many thousands of years ago. Maybe to the time you spoke of when you mentioned the Aztecs. Possibly even before that, too. Back to an age when a very advanced race lived on Earth. To a time when there was a warning of an impending catastrophe.

"The holocaust struck quickly, and those who were left made their home at the present South Pole. I would suggest that Queen Maud Land was their home. They settled down to rebuild their life as they had once known it, and as the years passed the cold began to recede, but not at the pole. There it remained frozen and desolate. It was there that this race of people began to wear clothing, and this was to keep their bodies warm, and not for the sake of modesty.

"After they had lived there for many years, and the cold had released the earth, except for the pole, another race arrived from far away, making the previous race their slaves. The newcomers were sadistic and lecherous, using the women as their toys, the men as their workers. The newcomers arrived here in the type of spacecraft we now see in our skies. For some reason they settled at the pole, shunning the outside world, maybe because of its lack of living things. An age passed by, and the children, born of the lecherous knowledge of the Earth women, became the masters. I refer to the male offspring, of course, and they continued their lustful actions upon the female offspring, producing more young. They worked and died, and the race continued. Maybe these people, if that is the correct term, are the lost race we have heard so much about.

"It is possible that they were the ones who built the pyramids, the ones who carved the huge monoliths on Easter Island. It is possible that here we have the two races referred to by Shaver. I believe too this theory would account for the reason that UFOs have been seen over many centuries. The one part that I have no answer for is, of course, why they haven't attacked us, taking over the earth."

As I spoke, I gradually came out of the "trance" I seemed to be under. Barbara apparently forgot about my strange manner, in her fascination for what I had been saying, for she broke in with a question.

"But why should they want to take over the earth, Johnnie?" she asked, a little fearfully.

"I'm not certain, Barbara. But the answer might be hidden behind a rather cryptic question, 'What color is Saturday?' And when you answer that, well, you might well have the answer to our puzzle."

"Yes, I see that. Now you say these people of the earth wore clothing only when they went to the pole. Do you mean that in their normal life, prior to the catastrophe, they went about naked?"

"Yes. And there may be some connection there between these people and Adam and Eve. Although it could be a very remote possibility," I explained. "There is no doubt that clothes were used in those far away days as a sort of decoration, and not to hide the human body as they are today. we read of the ancient Greeks stripping to take part in their athletic games, and this seems to show, quite obviously, that clothes were only a form of decoration. This is shown in the pictures found in the togas of Egypt. The slaves are depicted as naked, and in many cases, the daughters of the priests and other high-ranking ones, the pictures show a girl in a skirt-like garment. Her breasts are always bare. But returning to our earlier talk, the race which settled at the pole had no need for clothes, it not being until they settled at the pole that the need did arise."

"What about the girls," Barbara asked with concern. "Were they safe, do you think, without clothing?"

"I believe there was a law in their community which protected the women -- either a moral code or a punitive code. To have contravened it would have been a most serious thing. I believe this has something to do with the Biblical account of Adam and Eve."

"It could," agreed Barbara. "Now, what would you say as to how your ice people appear? What are they like in build? In general appearance?"

"The first race was like us. Just normal looking humans, but there could have been a nuclear explosion to have caused the catastrophe, and the blast could have changed their glands, and the functioning of them. Radiation could have made a lot of changes, and so could the attacking races who came later. As the women gave birth to their children, they produced something far different from themselves. The attacking race could have been something quite frightening to us of today, and definitely foreign to Earth people. I can picture something with a large head, a big body, and webbed feet."

"Why the webbed feet?"

"Because they lived, and still live, in the sea."
"Why the sea, though," Barbara asked.

"They probably lived in the sea back on their own planet before coming to Earth. They could have been half-man, if that is the word I want..."

"Like a satyr?" shuddered Barbara.

"Yes, like a satyr," I nodded. "And there again is another fairy tale which could have a basis in fact. The story of the satyrs and races, and the nymphs. Maybe the satyrs were the attacking nymphs were the Earth people."

"The nymphs always lost, didn't they?"

"Yes, the satyr always caught them. . . "

"What a horrible thought," Barbara whispered.

"One only need to look at Clodion's work of art 'Nymph and Satyr,' to appreciate what happened to the women when they were caught by the Satyrs. They were slaves to the things; Clodion's work is unmercifully explicit, as the nymph pours wine into the open mouth of her violator."

"And now we believe these two were those who once occupied the earth?"

"If you wish to let your imagination go that far, Barbs, I told her."

I remembered her asking for help the previous evening, as she asked, with some noticeable agitation, "Then you believe that these so-called fairy tales have a basis in fact?"

"I do," I said earnestly. "And I also believe that the controllers of most of the present UFOs are the descendants of those very ones the fairy tales tell us of. I say 'fairy tales,' meaning, naturally, stories which seem to belong in the realm of fantasy."

"This is all very interesting," Johnnie, she said in a quiet voice, "but rather frightening, just the same."

"Still want to be a UFO researcher?" I asked her lightly.

"YES!" was her emphatic reply.

Then she looked toward the floor, and said in a very low, halting, almost sobbing voice:

"Johnny, are you thinking...are you thinking that one of those blokes might...might rape me too!"

"Now, Barbara, that's too fantastic to entertain," I answered calmly and seriously.

She tried to smile. "I hope you're right, Johnnie."

## CHAPTER TEN
## THE VISITOR

I will not attempt to explain the happenings I will now relate. Perhaps one more versed than I in the fields of hidden knowledge may be able to make some pattern or sense out of it. I can only relate it the way it actually happened. I go back to a continuation of our discussion on the same evening.

"To continue with this theory," I stated, "the UFO characters keep in touch with the outside world by mental telepathy, and by that means they know just what we do, and what is happening on any given part of the earth. And it is through that means that some researchers have met with trouble."

"Al Bender, too?"

"In a way. But I reckon his visitors were as human as you and me. Maybe he had similar thoughts as ours...would you agree with that?"

"Yes," answered Barbara. "But where do these strange odors come into it all? The strange things we heard from America? What of them?"

(Editor's note: At the time this book was written by John Stuart, the book by Albert K. Bender had not yet been distributed — G.B.)

"Maybe it has something to do with a possibility that they travel via the astral plane. The smells...well, that could be their natural odor."

"But," remonstrated Barbara, "the idea that they might travel via the astral plane is getting very close to spiritualism."

"I know. But we are dealing with a race far in advance of us," I replied seriously.

"But, that means that old Satan is wrapped up in this business?" she cried out.

"Well, it is possible, too, Barbara. Anything is possible in this business." I tensed. I saw the sane hard look steal over Barbara's features which I had noticed the night before. Her innocent face steeled into a cold, sensuous thing.

"Anything is possible, eh?" she asked, teasingly; and then as a wild and tempestuous expression came in her eyes, she taunted, "Even letting me sit here unclothed?" She chuckled impishly. I was frightened.

"Later, eh?" I replied, not knowing quite what to say.

"I'll keep you to that," she murmured, almost happily.

I tried to get her mind off what certainly, I thought, must be some sort of an evil possession. I continued: "As I was saying, anything is possible. I too believe that the UFO controllers can project their inner-selves to any point they care to. It's easy, really, because I learned the use of such a power myself."

"You can what!" gasped Barbara, staring at me.

"Project my inner self to any point I wish," I explained. "I can sit here and, say, visit you. It's my inner—self which goes out."

"And you can see just as if you were really there?" "Gee," she grinned. "That'd be nice, wouldn't it?"

She laughed softly as if the idea were filled with some deep secret amusement.

"But coming back to Al Bender. Who were his visitors? Were they space men?"

"No," I explained, "I feel they were definitely human. They could have been from his own Government, or they might have been priests from some church or other. Either would interpret the fear he felt if his findings were against the safety of his country. And of the world, too, possibly."

"That means then that he may have had the actual solution to the UFOs?"

"Exactly, Barbara. If it's not the actual solution, then it must be something pretty big. But whatever he knew was sufficient to cause his silence, and sufficient to cause him to feel ill for some days after the visit."

"But," remarked Barbara, "If his theory was the correct one, why did it make him sick only after his visitors had left? Isn't it more likely that it was something he was told which made him ill? A warning of some sort? But I find it hard to interpret his sickness. (The strange sensuous look had now left Barbara's face). Why should it make him ill? Did his findings mean some shocking cruelty from the UFOs? Did the fear affect the safety of his wife?"

"Al was single when he said the three men visited him."

"No," Barbara went on, "there's a point there that we haven't got on to. I seem to feel it was something Bender just couldn't say, something he might even be ashamed to say. Something along the lines we have been talking about. I am certain of one thing – Bender is not a kook. He's telling the truth about being silenced, but he hasn't told everything and I don't think he EVER WILL tell everything."

"Whatever it was, Barb, it was pretty grim. Something he could not fight against, and something he would have to face helplessly," I added, as I looked at her.
"And you can rest in peace knowing that whatever it is we have to fear, I'll do all in my power to offer you protection, just as I would my own wife. If I can, as a man, stop your being harmed, then I'll do all possible."

Tears came to her eyes, as she said, "Thank you, Johnnie. It's nice to know you have said all that. I've never had any fears since we began this research, but the time might come when I'll know fear. But the fact that you are near to help will lighten the load that may weigh in my heart and upon my mind."

She wiped her eyes, and added, "I'll be all right, Johnnie. They won't try to harm me."

"They won't try to harm me." was this a deep faith she had in me? Or was it that she really felt that there were no dangers? Whatever she felt in her heart, it was wrong, for she was in danger. A shocking danger. But one we never foresaw, and therefore had no defense against. And as we did not know what those future days and nights held for us, we calmly went ahead with our research into the UFOs, carefully analyzing each report, adding more views and thoughts to our theory.

Prior to the first serious attack upon us, an incident took place which, like, so many others, is unexplainable. Although it was a much different type of interference from that which we would experience later, it is probably linked to the other matters and must therefore be added here. It was a warm evening, as I sat across from my companion, talking of the possibility that Mars might be involved in the UFO business.

When I saw Barbara suddenly stare, partly in fear, over my head, I turned and saw a stranger standing almost behind me, a soft smile on his rather effeminate face. I sprang to my feet, seeing that Barbara was sitting quite still. I asked the man who he was and how he got into my home? A soft smile was his reply, and at last he told us he was a space man, and had called to add his words to the warning I had received some months before.

I was shaken by this visit, and found myself just standing there, staring at and studying my visitor. I put his age at about 30 years. He was tall, and slimly built. But I was not fooled with this slim appearance, realizing that there were well-developed muscles beneath the black suit he wore. His skin was such that any girl would have been envious of it. He was tanned to a deep tan color, and his hair was quite long, being very fair. His eyes were a soft blue and held a friendly expression. It seemed that there was nothing to fear from him, and it was apparent that Barbara saw nothing to disturb her, for she still sat in her chair.

The stranger again told us to leave well enough alone, and to cease our investigations. His eyes moved to Barbara, and he pointed out that she would be in danger if we persisted. With this warning still in our ears, the stranger vanished from view. I poured two large brandies, and stared at my young companion. She was looking fixedly at the spot where the stranger had stood, her eyes filled with amazement. Then she turned to stare at me, and I saw her hand was shaking slightly. I suggested that she had better go home, and agreed to accompany her part of the way.

## CHAPTER ELEVEN
## THE SECRET OF THE SPHINX

The following evening we discussed the strange affair, and tried to explain it away to ourselves as a hoax or prank of some sort, but I'm afraid we were not successful.

Even as we talked, we both heard the distinct sound of a chuckle in the corner behind Barbara's chair. I spun to face that direction, but there was nothing, just the silence to mock us after the uncanny sound. We tried to settle down to the UFO problem again.

"Do you really believe that the people who built the pyramids are in the UFO game too?" she asked me.

"Yes, I do. While I was in Egypt I naturally went to see the pyramids, climbing to the top, both inside and outside. I found it all most interesting, and went to see the tombs which are down below the Sphinx. And in Cairo I came to know a young man who was a curate of the Egyptian Museum. I mentioned the Sun Stella to him."

"What is the Sun Stella, Johnnie," Barbara interrupted.

"It's a very large slab of sandstone which rests between the paws of the Sphinx. On it can be seen many hieroglyphics, which once were translated, but I cannot remember now what it all meant. However, I mentioned the Sun Stella to my good friend, and he nodded.

"'Yes, John, it is a genuine treasure. From it we have found much to explain the life of a past race. Of course you will know it conceals a door.'" "'A door? Where does it go to, George?'"

"'It conceals a door which gives access to a rather long passage beneath the Sphinx, which in turn leads to a secret chamber beneath the pyramid of Cheops.'"

I explained to Barbara that Cheops was the largest of the three pyramids.

"I asked George what this secret chamber was used for. He replied, 'It is not used these days, John. But it was used in a far away age when Amenhotep was Pharaoh. And beyond the wall of that chamber is yet another smaller one. And it is in that smaller chamber we find the secret of the earth's future.'"

"And what did he mean by the secret to our future, Johnnie?" asked Barbara.

"I asked him that, too, but he wouldn't tell me any more, although I felt, and still feel, that he knew a lot more than he told me. "And what would you say was in that smaller chamber?"

"I don't know, Barb. But I have an idea, though, and it is one which I wouldn't be game to speak of. It's too startling and fantastic," I told her quietly.

"Wouldn't you tell ME?" she inquired.

"Yes, one day soon I'll tell you."

The following days brought us many new reports, and among them were two from the South Island; but these were undoubtedly meteors. But the reports on them in the press proved just how simple it is to be confused with meteors and UFOs. Some of the descriptions: "A large object resembling an orange tennis ball; A bright wriggly thing with a trail of smoke stretched out behind a flying saucer; A weird ball of fire shooting sparks every where; A flaming mass shooting through the sky."

This, we admitted, was a case for the scoffers, and we knew how they would laugh their empty heads off, knowing too that these people would forget that the serious researcher had already dismissed the report as nothing more startling than a meteor.

"What would be the explanation of the scoffers regarding the objects seen at the NATO exercise?" I mused.

"Balloons," grinned Barbara.

"And how about this one? 'Strange Object Seen In Sky From City and Huntly.' Five people saw this, and it sounds like quite a good report. I suppose it was a balloon, though. Or it could be a piece of meteoric rock as was once claimed by our local astronomer, Mr. Bryce, eh?"

"What else is there, Johnnie?" laughed Barbara.

G. DUPLANTIER

"This one says that a strange object fell from the sky after three mysterious explosions. Wonder what it was?"

"That was Venus, Jonnnie, only the planet was having a bit of trouble," she laughingly remarked.

That was June, 1954. A beautiful evening. Clear and rather mild. The terror was closer to us now, and soon the pressure would increase to force us out of this research. But on this evening there was nothing to fear and we walked in the moonlight, still discussing the theory we had thought out.

We strolled along, lost in the world of mystery, and I was rather startled when Barbara suddenly came up with: "Do you really and honestly believe I am in danger from these things, Johnnie?"

"Yes," I answered grimly. "I do."

"And what are they likely to do to me?" she inquired, adding one terrible possibility.

I stopped and gripped her shoulders, staring down at her. "That could happen too!" I said harshly. "Doesn't that scare you?"

"I don't know, Johnnie," she replied. "I suppose that if it did happen I'd be terrified. But the thought doesn't worry me very much."

She grinned at my serious expression. "Anyway, nothing has happened to me yet, so why worry?"

"Nothing has happened yet!" I echoed. "Can't you realize what could happen to you?"

"Yes, I do, Johnnie. And I refuse to be frightened!" she replied with some spirit. Then she said, rather strangely, "But I might like to meet a space man. I wonder what one'd be like?"

"Stop it!"

"I think I'd kiss him, y'know," she said with a grin.

"You might get one heck of a shock if you did see one of these things!"

"Something like a satyr?"

"Yes."
"The satyr and the nymph. Me, of course, being the nymph?"

"Barbara, I can't understand your silly talk about this! You don't seem particularly concerned about it all, do you?"

"No. Why should I? I haven't been hurt yet, as I have already said, and should they attack me, well, that is when the time will come to worry."

Her attitude rather frightened me, and that evening when I said good night to her I again warned her to take care.

"Look, Johnnie. I'm all right. Now stop being a silly goat! I'm not going to be harmed."

She was soon lost in the darkness as she moved away.

## CHAPTER TWELVE
### I SEE THE DISC

I stood there, pondering her strange attitude, and wondered if she were as relaxed as she made herself appear to be. I didn't like it at all. The fear was growing in me that they would strike at her. Would I be able to protect her? What would happen? When would it happen?

I began to feel that the attack was coming, and beads of perspiration formed on my forehead as I thought of Barbara being used as a plaything of some heinous thing. I was trembling. With a cigarette lit I felt a little better, and my wife just arriving from her lodge meeting brought a happy smile on my face.

"Hullo, you're out late, boy."

"Yes. I was just thinking of the UFOs, darling. I don't know if we're making any progress, but it could be that we have stumbled on something pretty big. Dunno yet."

I threw my cigarette away and lit another, and the action did not escape my wife's attention.

"What are you worried about, John?"

"Nothing, dear," I lied. "Just tired, that's all.

I drew on my cigarette, and, looking up at the stars, remarked, "It's just the sort of evening to see a saucer. Y'know, darling, that's what I'd like to do."

"You've seen them before."

"I know. But I'd like to have a fair dinkum close look at one. Be rather interesting, wouldn't it?"

"For you and Barbara it would be very interesting. But I'm going to bed. Coming in?"

"Shortly, darling. I'll finish my cigarette before I do. Anyway, I may see a saucer."

G. DUPLANTIER

I leaned against the gate staring upward, still thinking of Barbara's strange manner. I tried to force it from me, but the feeling persisted in my mind. She was in danger. But how to make her realize it?

I wasn't going to accept her claim that there was no fear in her mind that she would be attacked; but if such an attack did take place, what would happen. What force would be used? And what form would an attack take? Would it affect her sanity? Would she still be able to carry on our research? A thousand similar questions raced through my mind. Did she really have fears that an attack would take the form she suggested? It was almost too frightening to think about! But the fact remained that she thought they would attack her in such fashion. What if this should come about when I wasn't present? How could I protect her then?

My thoughts were interrupted by a light. I straightened up. It was very high and moving slowly. North to south. It must be all of 10,000 feet, I thought. It was now at an angle of about 70 degrees to my eyes.

Quite big, really. Not a meteor -- not moving fast enough. It stopped, as I watched with some excitement. Now it was growing bigger and had changed from a reddish- orange to a duller yellow. Still very bright, though. Still bigger. I could now make out its shape. Bell-like. Still a dullish yellow. It was now down to about 200 feet! And still descending.

It descended to about 100 feet above me, or maybe a little higher. I stared at it. It was rocking slightly. I estimated it was about 30 feet across, and maybe slightly higher from rim to the round ring I could see on top. Up near the top of the object was a row of circular portholes, and from these a bright light shone.

It was pulsating a little, while a band, containing the ports, revolved slowly. Underneath I was able to make out three ball things, which I decided could be its landing gear. At the height where it was I decided it was a dark grey in color, although it was hard to be definite. I detected no sound from the object, but after it had hung there for about ten minutes (this again is difficult to be certain of, owing to the excitement I felt}, it suddenly rose to a great height and raced away to the south.

I stood there, trying to collect my excited thoughts, and made myself realize that I had seen a UFO at very close quarters. I was sorry that my wife hadn't hear me call to her. I hurried inside to tell my wife of what I had just seen, and my excitement was sufficient to prove to her that there certainly had been something there. I was very keen to find a witness, and discovered that there was one! I was safe now from ridicule.

The next night I related the details of the sighting to Barbara, and she questioned me closely. She was most convinced that I had actually seen it. We then returned to our Antarctica theory, this in turn brought us back to Bender's affair, and after discussing our previous view, we turned to Edward Jarrold of Australia.

"Who was Ed's visitor," she asked.

"He might have been from Australian Air Force Intelligence," I replied. "He did tell us in his letter that he was onto something pretty big, and that he had been invited to meet a bloke from R.A.A.F. Intelligence. And you remember we have his report on the meeting. No, I don't believe it was an official from Air Force, Barb."

"H'm. Well, who the blue blazes was the bloke?" she asked impatiently.

"Haven't a clue on that one, I'm afraid."

"Harold Fulton might know, mightn't he?"

"Granted. But we can't ring Harold up and say, 'Look, Harold, old boy, who was Ed's visitor?' Can we?"

"Oh I know that, you idiot."

"Well, what can we do?"

Barbara shook her head. "Oh, I suppose we will have to leave it for the moment, eh? Let's have another look at this area..."

She stopped suddenly to look across the room with a strained expression. A frown crossed her face, and then her eyes turned to mine. I had also heard it. A kind of whisper.

I felt that it came from somebody who had been listening to our conversation, and had whispered some comment to it! I was ready to face anything I could see, but when it came to something invisible, I didn't feel so confident! I tensed as Barbara held my arm in her hand, her startled whisper breaking the tension.

"What...was it, Johnnie?"

I sensed the fear she felt, and to calm her nerves, I tried to laugh, failing miserably.

"Oh...I reckon we were just hearing things, my dear."

Her eyes roved the room, and she asked grimly, "Were we?"

Her hand was shaking as she held out her cigarettes. I took one and flicked my Ronson.

"I'm frightened, Johnnie!"

"But I'll look after you, Barbara," I said, hoping my words would calm her.

"I...I...let me sit near you."

She moved her chair next to mine and I put my arms around her waist, feeling her trembling body. Did we hear the sound, or was it just a case of hearing things? Had just one heard the whisper, it would be different, but we had both heard it.

"What is it, John?" she asked fearfully. Have we discovered something? Something we aren't supposed to know? Is that it?" she asked me, her eyes demanding an answer.

"Yes," I admitted wearily, "I do believe we know more than is safe for us."

## CHAPTER THIRTEEN
## THE HIDEOUS THING

"Look, Barbara, you've got to get out before it's too late!" I warned. "It's you they'll hurt. You're a girl!"

"I refuse to give up!" she told me firmly, and again her eyes widened. Her slim body stiffened.

"What...what was that?" she whispered. A distinct sound of breathing came from across the room! And it sounded as if the breather had a serious case of asthma. Then it stopped, and I nervously lit a cigarette, not knowing quite how to tackle a problem such as this.

I didn't try, for I realized I was doomed to failure before I even started. But my companion was afraid now, and her earlier words were forgotten.

It was quite early when I said goodnight to her at the gate, my mind filled with thoughts of danger for her. This fear was to grow in intensity as the days went by, and would continue until the first of the horrifying attacks, only then to become greater! What was to be next? Had we known, F.S.I. would have closed down there and then, forgetting that there were UFOs to be studied. But we didn't know.

So far the attacks, if they were caused by our research, had not been too serious. They had shaken us considerably, a lot more than I was prepared to admit. I was almost at the stage where I was looking over my shoulder at each step. My health began to suffer. Barbara looked wan and tired, and I knew she was afraid, too. But we persisted in our research, and soon were to be sorry that we had not heeded the warnings.

The terror was about to strike! That Friday evening was much the same as any other, though I later felt most thankful that my wife had been out with a girl friend. Barbara and I settled down to talk; then soon afterward she realized she was out of cigarettes and decided to go to the store after a pack.

I got myself a pot of beer, and sat down with it. The "sounds" still concerned me. I glanced at my watch. Ten minutes. I continued to think. Another look. Twenty minutes had passed, and still there was no sign of Barbara. I became anxious about her safety.

Another look at my watch, and still another. By then I was very anxious. I got up and started to walk back and forth across the lounge. Suddenly the front door flew open, and a figure rushed into my arms.

Barbara said in a voice filled with fear, "There's something out there!"

Quickly releasing her, I hurried outside, stopping on the top step as a terrible stench struck me. I almost fainted in terror. It was like burnt plastic and sulphur. I stood there for a moment, and then walked down to the front gate, neither seeing nor hearing anything. I retraced my steps, seeing Barbara was on the upper step, watching me. I searched the rear of the grounds, finding nothing, and had just started to return to the door when I heard distinct sounds behind me. I stopped and shone my torch. There was nothing there.

I walked on. The sounds followed. I stopped and the sound stopped. I moved. It moved. Again I stopped, was amazed and startled when "it" kept on! The peculiar shuffling, scraping sound went past me, and I felt something solid brush against my shoulder!

This was the first indication I'd had that "they" were solid as I! As the sound continued toward the front gate, I slowly walked to the door, joining Barbara. I asked her if she had heard it.

"Yes, Johnnie. It was the same as I heard outside when I came from getting the cigarettes."

I saw fear living in her eyes and I wanted to send her away. But now it was too late. I poured two brandies, and told her I was going out for another look around.

"I'm coming, too, Johnnie," she told me firmly.

I shook my head. "You're going to stay here!"

She came closer, and tried to smile. "But, if I'm with you, Johnnie, I'll be safer than here on my own. won't I?" she asked with logic.

"All right," I agreed. "Only stay close to me!"

"Yes, Johnnie," she said, a little meekly.

I felt her hand on my arm as I walked along the path to the rear of the house. I turned the corner, stopping in horror, feeling, more than seeing, Barbara move to my side.

We stared at the evil thing which faced us about 27 feet across the lawn. It was loathsome. Hideous. Evil. Disgusting. Horrifying.

It was about eight feet in height. I don't profess to be a hero, nor am I a coward, but this thing was sufficient to cause me a lot of natural fear. We stood transfixed, staring in complete horror at the monster in the exceptionally bright moonlight.

I felt a desire to take Barbara and run as fast as possible from it, but I discovered I had no will-power to move a finger. I was helpless! I forced myself to pay some attention to its appearance, wanting to hold my companion close in protection, for even at that moment I had some premonition of what was to come.

The monster's head was large and bulbous. No neck. A huge and ungainly body supported on ridiculously short legs. It had webbed feet. The arms were thin and not unlike stalks of bamboo. It had no hands, the long fingers jutting from the arms like stalks. Its eyes were about four inches across, red in color. There was no nose, just two holes, and the mouth was simply a straight slash across its appallingly lecherous face.

The whole was a green lime in color, and it was possible to see red veins running through its ungainly form. The monster was definitely male. Barbara's eyes opened wide in fear and shocking horror at the sight of this monster.

She was not moving in any way, and I felt she was held powerless as was I. We were at the mercy of the odiously base thing. I almost wept with distracted terror, as I understood the intentions of the hideous thing. I strove frantically to move, inwardly moaning that I was held in the power of the terror before us.

It was now moving toward us, its filthy eyes fixed on Barbara's slim body. I shuddered. Completely frantic now, I tried to pray, but the words just wouldn't form in my mind.

G. DUPLANTIER

Still closer, its spindly arms lifted toward her body. I felt the sweat trickle down my face, my chest and my back. The fingers were now almost touching her shirt. I tried to yell her name as Barbara seemed to come into complete mental control of the monster, and I will spare the reader Barbara's actions.

This wasn't my little friend! She was a stranger! She had to be! She seemed to be waiting for the filthy hands to touch her! The arms lifted more and only a hair's breadth now separated her body from its fingers. I saw all this in the moonlight as I watched helplessly, knowing I couldn't stop it carrying out its hideous attack. I could only watch in terror.

It was our master and it was making Barbara obey its instructions. It was the only answer! It had to be the answer. But just at what seemed to be the critical moment, the thing withdrew its hands from her and moved slowly back to where it had been standing when we first saw it.

Then it disappeared from sight. Barbara moaned and fell into my arms, and she shook uncontrollably. I got her into the lounge, eased her into a chair and got her some brandy.

Her lips were moving, but there was no sound. I knelt in front of her, holding her hands, feeling with my free one for some cigarettes.

"What....what was it, Johnnie?" she whispered in terror.

"God above knows, dear! I don't!"

She nodded slowly, and then said in a strained voice, "You saw...what it made me do?"

Tears overflowed now, and her young body shook.

"Yes," I told her miserably, "I know."
"I'll be all right, Johnnie," she whispered. "I got a fright, that's all."

"I'll take you home, Barbara."

She nodded. "Home. Home to what, Johnnie?" She smiled grimly.

"Home to another attack? Maybe it will come back. Yes," she continued as if in a daze, "it might come back again. This time I won't escape from it."

Her words stopped as she saw the expression of terrible fear in my eyes.

"Please, Johnnie," she whispered. "Nothing is going to happen.

"I'm not leaving you alone!"

"It won't come back. Take me home," she asked. "You certainly can't spend the night in my room," she grinned bravely. "Look, Johnnie, I'll be safe. Dinkum, I will."

"All right. Come on."

I walked along with her, amazed at her efforts to sound quite normal as she chattered to me. It was an act. But a very brave one. She swung her hand as it gripped mine, and said brightly, "I'd like to kiss you, Johnnie. Shall I?"

"Would that make you feel any better?"

"Very much better," and she pulled my head down and kissed me on the cheek warmly.

At the house I had to leave her alone, but the rest of the night was long, and sleep was far away from me. I was too afraid that the telephone would ring and I wouldn't hear it. At last, though, dawn broke and the birds sang as I told my wife of the shocking attack.

After breakfast I sat in my chair, my thoughts chaotic and grim, and later I sat on the front step. Questions tumbled through my mind with a speed that left me breathless. What was it? Where did it come from? Why did it attack us? What was behind it? Would it return? Was Barbara safe from another attack? How could I protect her?

I lit another cigarette and walked to the corner, staring across the lawn to where it had stood, almost again seeing it, in my mind's eye. I shuddered and returned to the steps, still deep in thought.

I jumped as a voice greeted me, and I looked up at the strangely beautiful girl who faced me, a look of curiosity in her lovely eyes.

"Hullo, Terry," I smiled and rose to my feet. "You're very grave this morning, John," she said in her lilting voice, and sat on the step.

"I...I would like to talk to you. Do you mind?"

"I feel deeply honored that you have joined me, fair lady," I murmured sincerely.

She appeared nervous, and at last sari, hesitantly, "John ...Would....oh! Listen, did you see anything on your back lawn last evening?" she hurriedly asked.

I stiffened and lit a cigarette, lifting my head in surprise. "What was there?" I asked tensely.

She drew a small pad from her pocket and quickly sketched. She handed it to me. "This!"

I stared at the very same "green thing" Barbara and I had seen. Terry had drawn a remarkable likeness, almost as hideous as the actual thing. Hardly a detail was missing, and I knew she had seen the same thing.

"We both saw it, Terry. It...it was absolutely hideous," I said, forcing the words from my tight throat.

I told her what had occurred, right from the start, and found it made me feel much better.

"It was going to...do something awful to Barbara," she gasped in horror, her slim hand on my arm.

"Yes, Terry, that is about what it was going to do when whatever controlled it, and God knows what that was, called it back from her. I was in a terrible fever the whole time, and did everything I knew how to break the power it held me under. I had to stand there and watch it all."

I felt ill at the memory.

"Where were you?"

"Just around the corner, Terry. That's why you couldn't see us, although you could see the monster on the lawn."

"It didn't hurt Barbara?" Terry asked in sincere concern.

"She was terribly afraid after it was over, but there was no physical harm," I told her.

Then I added, "Fortunately!"

"Yes, fortunately," she said softly.

Soon after that she left me, and I watched as she walked quietly along the path. I returned to my thoughts and soon saw Barbara smiling down at me.

## CHAPTER FOURTEEN
## THE CREATURE RETURNS

"Hullo, Johnnie. You look all in," Barbara greeted me.

"You are the one who should be ill, Barbara, but I feel terrible."

"You look it, too, John! Did you tell your wife?"

"Yes. I told her as I lay in bed at dawn. It was so strange to be telling her of the terror while outside the birds sang happily. Nothing further happened to you? No troubles?"

"None, Johnnie," she told me. "I took some aspirin and went to bed. I slept right through the night." (She didn't tell me that she had taken so many tablets that she had put herself into a drugged sleep. I did not learn that until much later.)

"Terry came over to see me this morning. She saw the thing too."

Barbara gasped. "She. . .saw it too?" Her eyes were wide. "But...if she saw the thing, she must have seen everything!"

"No, she wasn't able to see us. Just the thing."

"Strike! What a shock for little, sweet Terry."

I nodded. "Yes, it was a shock, but it didn't stop her from making a sketch of it. Every detail was there, and it proved that she saw it."

"Strewth!" was Barbara's reply. "What a girl!"

We talked about the thing because it had to be discussed. We had to talk about it to find some answer, to find some defense against another similar episode.

"Well, as Terry saw the thing, it proves it was there, doesn't it? It was fair dinkum, alright," nodded my companion.

"Of course it was fair dinkum! It wasn't a nightmare we had last night, girl!"

I almost yelled at her. "And, my dear, you're going to pull out before it's too late!"

Her head turned, and she stared at me in amazement.

"I'm going to . . . what?" she gasped. "Look, if you think I'm going to be scared out of this business, you've got to think again! I'm in this, and in it I'm going to stay!"

She lit herself a fresh cigarette. "Pull out! Just because that ugly thing appeared and did what it did! It's not enough to frighten me out of all this! I'm not a coward!" She almost shouted.

"I didn't say you were a coward! But I'm not going to stand by and see the same thing happen again!"

She looked down at her cigarette. "I'm sorry, Johnnie! You couldn't have helped me, even though you had tried."

This was in answer to the inference that I stood by and couldn't help her. I knew we hadn't seen the last of this thing, and I knew somehow that she would be in danger again. I was terribly afraid for her safety, but deeply shocked as I saw again and again that I would be powerless to save her.

Whatever we might have anticipated regarding the next attack, it should have been what actually happened! It was one affair I will always remember for its ferocity, and for the harm they did to my young friend. I know that somewhere in our research we stumbled onto the truth, and they were determined to frighten us sufficiently so that we would be silent.

I pointed this out to Barbara a number of times over the following evenings, but she was adamant that we were going to carry out our efforts. As she gradually recovered from her terrible fright, we found we could discuss the attack with a calm outlook -- but we never did arrive at any particular answers.

Then, one evening, just before the end came, I again escorted Barbara home, amused at her chatter of happiness. There was nothing in the air to show us there was anything to fear, and she even facetiously remarked that one evening perhaps she would meet a space man in her room. I told her not to talk like that, but she only laughed delightedly.

At her door, however, it was different, and she asked me to search the room for her. I found nothing, and it wasn't until the following day that I remembered the very slight, but most peculiar odor I had detected. There had been the usual feminine odor of powders, perfumes and the usual makeup, and these registered in my mind. But there had also been the other smell, like burned plastic or sulphur.

My overlooking this was a terrible mistake, for it was that night when they struck again. And they struck while she was alone!

I left her and walked home, unaware as I lay in bed reading that she was undergoing a terror such as a human had never known! And it was not until many hours later that I learned of the hideous attack they launched upon this defenseless girl. When I did learn about it, I marveled at the manner in which she managed to retain her sanity in spite of the horrors she had known.

I saw her the following day, and was uneasy when I detected she was walking in some sort of daze — or a horror-filled dream. And that evening she told me all that had befallen her after I left her alone.

I saw the vile scene as she spoke! A terrible coldness gripped my stomach, and I wondered how any girl could have endured such horror and remained sane!

She sat at my side, her hand resting on mine, and there was a slight trembling, but her voice was surprisingly calm. She seemed to be quite unmoved, but I was aware that she was on the verge of hysterical tears.

After she had related the ghastly details of the attack, she typed a report on it in ghastly completeness. I read it. It was all there. A shocking testimony of fear!

I will abridge this report in presenting it to the reader, for only a few could peruse it without becoming ill — if it were presented as Barbara wrote it: "When I entered my room last evening I immediately noticed a peculiar odor, but decided it came from outside. Also I did not want to mention this to Johnnie for fear it would unduly alarm him. I undressed and drew on my dressing gown, planning to have a bath before retiring. On my return from bathing, I removed my gown and sat down on my bed to smoke a cigarette. It was a very warm night.

"Suddenly I had the impression that I was not alone, that unseen eyes were studying me. This impression was so strong that I searched the room, finding nothing. I returned to sit on the bed, and to go over in my mind some of the research John and I were doing. The impression of unseen eyes persisted, but I forced myself to ignore it, preferring to think of our investigative tasks.

"I crushed my cigarette out and turned to pick up my pajamas, freezing as someone touched my shoulder. I jerked upright, my eyes closed in fear. I found that I was unable to move. I gradually mustered the will power to force my eyes open to see my attacker, I almost fainted away! I could see nobody in the room! Whatever or whoever it was, it was invisible!

"Hours seemed to pass, during which time I seem to be able to remember all details. I tried to think of my friend, John, and his grin, but all I could think of was the horror that I was experiencing.

"Finally the horror was gone. The attack ceased as suddenly as it had begun. I dragged myself to a sitting position and stared at my body, shuddering as I saw the fine scratches I was covered with. With a trembling hand I lit a cigarette and looked at my watch. Two and a half hours had passed! I tried to think clearly, and eventually forced my mind to accept what had happened to me. Sleep was far away and I tried to find an answer to this new development in the UFO research I had embarked upon.

"I concluded that the thing had been solid, even if invisible. There was, of. course, no way of knowing exactly what it was like, and I tried to form a picture in my mind to fit it, but I gave up in fear. I got into bed and eventually fell into a deep sleep filled with nightmares. With the light of day, I again looked at my body and shuddered when I saw the scratches. It had really happened after all! I felt sick, but I knew I would have to go to work, for to remain in my room all day would drive we completely mad!"

I listened to all Barbara told me in silence, almost petrified with horror at the bestial terror she had experienced at the hands of this invisible thing. I was not particularly keen to question her, but realized it was the only way we might solve the identity of the thing.

When I asked her if she felt well enough to answer some questions, she nodded. "Yes, Johnnie, I'm ready."

"What size would you estimate the thing to have been?"

"Much taller than you. Well over six feet or more."

And in reply to the texture of its skin, she replied, "It was like sandpaper. Very rough."

"Did you notice any particular odor?"

"About the same as we noticed the evening we saw the green thing. A little."

"Would you say it was anything like the green thing?"

"I couldn't say. It was invisible."

"Was there any sound?"

"None. Except for my own breathing."

"Did you notice any shadows?"

"Yes, when I first opened my eyes I saw a faint shadow against the wall at the head of my bed. It was a shadow of a man, only it was clearer below the waist."

"You had no trouble in seeing this?"

"None, because I was partly facing that way."

"You say you attempted to force it from you. Will you show me your hands? Palms up?" (I looked at her hands there were fine scratches covering the skin.) "I see." I watched as she stood up, pulling her shirt free from the waist band of her slacks.

"What are you doing, Barbara?" I asked her apprehensively.

"Forgive me, John, but this is something you must see!"

She faced me, calm, unmoving, and I stared at her, appalled at the scratches which covered the most of her body. I looked at her ribs closely, noting two brown marks about the size of an American 10-cent coin.

I mentioned these, and she told me, "They appeared there after the thing left, Johnnie. I don't know what caused them."

She slowly dressed and sat down again, her voice now telling of the fear she felt. "What was it, Johnnie?" She almost whispered. "Why did it do it?"

"God above knows that, my dear," I replied a little lamely. "Just one last question," I added. "You say it seemed to be only clinically interested in you, despite what it did? When did you get that impression?"

"It didn't seem to be very sensual. Just curious, that's all."

During the following weeks I saw the fight had died within her, and I knew there was little hope of our continuing this research to which we had dedicated ourselves. The months had taken their toll of me, too, and the fears that had known, the strain of too little sleep, had combined to undermine my health.

I realized the time had come to rest completely. Only after such a rest would I be able to return to my investigations with any vigor. Barbara informed me she was returning to her home, and I encouraged this, for to have made her change her mind could have been fatal to her. I felt lost without her to talk to, but I told myself I would return to the research alone. But it was not to be. "They" were to have the final word in this strange drama.

## CHAPTER FIFTEEN
## THE ENDING

For two days after Barbara's departure I rested, trying to forget the terrible experience she had endured, and then I felt an urge to make one further attempt to find some solution to the problem of Antarctica.

I had no idea of just how I would know if I did find a solution, but anything would be better than doing nothing at all. I surrounded myself with papers, reports, notes, our huge map and my reference books. I worked hard, analyzing reports, studying each minutely in the hope that something would give me a new lead. But each minute brought back the vision of Barbara's scratched body, and I felt a fear grow that I was only asking for more trouble.

I knew that by this disregard of the warnings I could be putting my wife in danger. I thought they would move against me first, for there was nothing my wife knew of the affair, apart from details of the attacks already made. This made me feel better, and I returned to my work.

The morning sped by. I was no further advanced. Lunch was over, and I returned to poring over the map, tensing when the doorbell rang. It was Terry. I sat at my desk, looking at this strangely lovely young girl. Twenty-one. Tall, for a girl. Slim, with a superb figure. Graceful as the legendary Diana. I had a deep respect for her, and usually felt that I was in the presence of a young Greek Goddess when she called to talk. I studied her as she relaxed in a deep chair, her soft hair forming a halo for her lovely face.

"It's nice of you to call, Terry," I said quietly. "May I get you a drink?"

"Thank you, John," she murmured, her blue eyes smiling with some inner amusement. She carefully lit one of her cigarettes with real rose petal tips and glanced at the huge map.

"What are all those lines, for?" she asked.

I explained the map, told her briefly of what we had been working on before our troubles.

"Will Barbara be joining you today?"

"Barbara's gone home," I replied. "She had a terrible experience a few weeks ago, and it was too much for her. She threw it in."

I was afraid she would question me about what had happened and I lit another cigarette to cover my nervousness.

"What happened, John?"

"Believe me, Terry, when I say it was a shocking matter that is about all I can tell you!"

"Why? I'm broadminded, John."

"It's all in a report she wrote up, but I'm afraid it would shock and frighten you."

"Why does everyone treat me like a child?" she exclaimed petulantly.

"You treat me as if I were some goddess out of a page in Greek mythology, John!"

I took Barbara's report from the pile of papers at my side, nervously handed it to her and watched her start to read. As she read her brow first wrinkled, and then I could see shocked amazement in her eyes. She completed it and looked up.

"It must have been terrible for Barbara," was her only comment.

"Yes, I saw the scratches this thing left on her, and I know Barbara told the truth."

"But why didn't you heed the warnings you had been given. You should have known better than to pursue this matter so far!"

"Maybe I didn't take them seriously."

"And the result was that?" She paused..."We have this report. And yet, in spite of that, you're still working on this strange thing?"

"Yes,"

"Have you ever thought that you might be fighting against the forces of Satan?"

This question was unlike Terry. She continued, "No, I'm not a religious crank! And I am trying to be serious!"

"The idea did occur to me once, but I refused to believe it."

"And after this thing happened to Barbara at her home, you still refuse to believe it?"

"I don't know what to think, Terry."

"What about your wife? Aren't you afraid these things might attack her?" she asked quietly.

"I don't believe she knows enough to be troubled."

She smoothed her hands over her modest skirt. "In your place, John, I'd be very worried."

She stood up and smiled down at me, and I rose. "You're playing with a dangerous weapon. Why not give up?" she asked very seriously.

"I will." I looked at the map. "Yes, it is a dangerous weapon to toy with, isn't it? There mightn't be any more warnings."

I drew on my cigarette. "Why the bloody hell didn't she listen to me? I told her to give up! But she refused to stop And the result was..."

I stopped because I didn't want to think about it. After she had left, I returned to my research and the hours fled by. I emptied my ashtray many times. I looked at my watch. 1:30 A.M. Time to stop. Time to go to bed. It sounded good to get some rest.

I looked up quickly. Tense. Nervous. That Sound! I rose and decided to look outside. I heard it again. I didn't like it. It came again. A sound too hard to describe. One which made my hair almost stand on end.

I wiped my brow. The room was turning cold on this summer night, or I was in a cold sweat. I knew there was some evil force present and I felt fear go down my spine. I looked about me. And then I saw "it"!

The thing was about four or five feet away from me. It was facing me in all its vile, base hideousness. Its body resembled, vaguely, that of a human. From the waist up it was a man, and from the waist down that of a woman.

Its flesh, stinkingly putrid, seemed to hang in folds. It was a grayish color. Evil exuded from the entire thing. The slack mouth was dribbling, and the horrible lips began to move, but there was no sound.

I realized with a shock that it was talking to me, using telepathy to converse. I was being warned not to proceed any further with my research. It seemed to laugh at me, and told of how others had suffered because they had attempted to solve the enigma, others like Barbara!

It told me, ***"Your friend knew too much and had to be silenced. We sent one of us to her as a warning. We weren't ready to allow it to complete its task at that time..."***

The thing told me in obscene words what Barbara had experienced, and each word was accompanied with what seemed to be laughter.

I abridge this "conversation" somewhat in the telling of it here. I asked, mentally, "How many were present?"

***"Thirteen of us. Only three were actually involved."***

"Why did you scratch her?"

***"It was something we couldn't avoid."***

"Where did the two brown marks come from?"

*"They are there to remind her of us,"* the thing again told me by telepathy.

At that point the thing seemed to waver, and grow less distinct; then materialized again into solidity. I almost collapsed in horror and revulsion as the male and female areas of its body had suddenly changed places.

*"You have been warned! Take heed! Should you fail there will be others to suffer!"*

Slowly it moved closer.

*"You have told another of your research. Tell her no more! Or we will have our revenge upon her! You understand?"*

The thing gloated, its slack mouth dribbling sickeningly.

"Terry!" I cried out.

*"That is what we know you to call her. She too will suffer if you are foolish!"*

"Why harm her?" I asked harshly. "She has nothing to do with my research!"

*"Already she knows what you have told her!"* It lifted its hands a little. *"If you persist, you will soon see what we can do!"*

Its foul eyes were now like chips of granite. Shortly it began to waver; then it just dissolved and was gone.

It had warned me to leave alone or else! I now saw fully the dangers I was against and broke into a cold sweat.

Why had they now selected Terry as their victim? I felt thankful that they had not threatened my wife. She knew as much as I.

Was it because of the gold cross she wore around her neck? Might that not be a protection? But the danger clearly wasn't worth it, and I knew the end of my research had indeed arrived. I would have to quit. I would go away on a holiday.

I went away to Auckland and stayed with my old mother, resting my nerves, trying to bring my shocked system back into order. The strain of the days behind weighed heavily upon me.

As I lay in the sun, trying to forget, the vision of the green thing returned to taunt me, and again I could visualize the scratches on poor Barbara's body. And there was nobody to tell of the experiences, so it would remain locked away in my tortured mind.

I couldn't even write and tell Gray Barker. I wondered what he would say if I sent a letter relating the final happenings. No, it couldn't be done. But he had to be warned of the danger behind this research.

I did finally decide to write him, but to alter the circumstances and still warn him. I want it known that ever since that day I have regretted this evasion. Gray had always been a sincere friend, and I should have realized at the time that he would have accepted that which was really the truth.

I do not yet fully understand the strange circumstances and phenomena which I ran against in the course of my research, and, when I wonder about this, and realize that I deliberately gave an altered version of what actually happened both to Gray Barker and to Harold Fulton,

I also wonder about other researchers and if the information they have given out to explain their "hushups" could have been, through reason of their best judgments, also altered somewhat.

I think that this unpleasant and frightening account should be ended as soon as possible, so I will be brief: Two years later I returned home and heard the malicious lies which had been spread regarding me. One of the lies claimed I had "gone away with the girl," and there were other stupidities.

I did turn back to my research, but my heart wasn't with it. I wasn't able to overlook the previous warnings. I knew my wife was too important to me to take any further risks; she was more to me than solving the enigma of the "flying saucers." And with that thought in mind, I quietly got down my research notebooks, and on the covers of each, below the name of the organization I added a notation:

**"CLOSED"**

# UFO WARNING

# By JOHN STUART

# ILLUSTRATED

# RETURN OF THE MEN IN BLACK BY TIMOTHY GREEN BECKLEY

You might think that true stories of the Men In Black are "old hat" (black ones at least I would hope!). That outside of an appearance on the silver screen at your local cinema, they have come and gone like will of the wisps, a part of UFO history that almost seems like it never happened at all.

BUT IT DID! AND THE FREIGHTENING ENCOUNTERS CONTINUE!

I should know as I have written more about the subject than anyone else that I know of.

My book THE UFO SILENCERS has gone into numerous editions and I have been quizzed on radio and television continuously because I have been credited with taking the only authentic photo of one of these menacing UFOlogical phantoms.

My most recent public proclamation about the MIB was made on the cable show UFO HUNTERS on the History Channel. I received quite a few e mails after my appearance (the show is still being aired worldwide) from individuals who finally had verification of their own encounters with these not so friendly entities from only the Lord knows where.

The following is an article that ran on over 40 blogs. Written by Sean Casteel it was originally posted on www.UFODigest.com and spread like internet wildfire. as if it were sweeps week.

## Timothy Beckley Goes On The Trail Of The Dreaded Men-In-Black With The UFO Hunters by Sean Casteel

**An Exclusive Interview With "Mr. UFO" As He Hits The Dusty Road In Search Of MIBs "UFO Hunters," The Silencers Episode, Air Date: October 29, 2009 On the History Channel**

What do we really know about the fabled and mysterious Men-In-Black? Perhaps the best person to ask is longtime veteran of the UFO wars Timothy Green Beckley, whose book on the subject is nowadays considered the definitive work on the bizarre "heavies" of Ufology. And who should ask Beckley for his informed take on the subject but Bill Birnes and the team behind the popular History Channel program **UFO Hunters**.

In a recent interview conducted for this site, Beckley filled in some of the background on his upcoming appearance.

"Several months ago," he said, "I was contacted by the History Channel, the producers of the *UFO Hunters* show. They were interested in doing an episode on the Men-In-Black. Now it turns out that the episode is titled "*The Silencers*," and of course the name of the book I wrote on the MIBs is titled *The UFO Silencers: Mystery of the Men in Black*. So that's a good thing for both them and me. It's sort of a built-in tag line to promote the book I did, which has become a classic in Ufology being that it is the only legitimate overview of the subject of these dark-suited individuals who have threatened eyewitnesses, contactees and abductees."

Along with contributing his own expertise, as well as what he says is the only authentic photograph of a real Man-In-Black (about which more later), Beckley also helped the show line up some additional guests.

"I suggested they reach out," Beckley said, "to several other people who had been harassed by these cloak-and-dagger-like individuals and strongly recommended they get in touch with a gentleman by the name of Johnny Sands, if it was humanly possible to locate him after all these years. The truth is, I hadn't heard from Johnny since his original experience took place toward the latter part of December, 1975. Johnny Sands has been for many years a country and western singer and a stuntman and an illusionist and magician who had a very interesting experience while driving towards Las Vegas.

"He was within view of the city lights," Beckley continued, "so he couldn't have been that far out of town, although the lights up and down the Vegas strip certainly do illuminate for many, many miles into the surrounding desert. Johnny says he was driving towards the city to see one of the agents who books acts for the lounge at this particular casino. Johnny had just come out with a new record and wanted to get a gig doing a live concert at this particular venue. He was anxious to get into town before it got too late and was disturbed by the fact that his engine seemed to be sputtering."

Sands next observed a strange light and his vehicle came to a complete stop. Two beings appeared, descending on a shaft of light. One of the beings stood off in the distance, while the other one approached Sands and his stalled automobile. Sands later told investigators that the beings were about 5 feet 8, were completely bald and had what appeared to be gills instead of ears.

"For the next ten minutes or so," Beckley went on, "they had a brief telepathic conversation about the lights off in the distance, what people did there. The beings produced a holographic image of the Earth, showing Sandy what appeared to be explosions taking place around the miniature globe, indicating perhaps some future global conflict. Finally, the beings got back into their ship, which then shot straight up."

About as typical as typical gets with a UFO encounter. But there was more, according to Beckley.

"The tie-in with the *UFO Hunters* show on *The Silencers*," Beckley explained, "is that Sands later had a rather hair-raising incident with the Men-In-Black who took him into the desert where he was confronted literally by a small army of more MIBs and two hairy creatures that reminded him of Cousin It from the *Addams Family Show*. I was always fascinated with Johnny's claims especially since he passed a lie detector test and had undergone a psychological examination by a trained professional, and I thought it would make a good addition to the *UFO Hunters* episode that was in the early planning stages."

The producers of the program, however, were unable to track Sands down and told Beckley they believed the gentleman had died some five years ago. The news greatly saddened Beckley, but then an interesting moment of synchronicity took place. Beckley went to visit his friend, a performance artist known professionally as *Zamora The Torture King*, who was doing a show on Coney Island near Beckley's home in Manhattan.

"I happened to mention," Beckley recalled, "since both of them are from the Las Vegas area, that I had tried to get in touch with Johnny Sands to get him on the History Channel and they had told me he had passed away. Zamora got a big chuckle out of that. 'Well, I don't think so,' he said, 'because I just interviewed him recently for my book *Weird Nevada*.' So it turns out that the producers of the show did finally manage to get in touch with Johnny and booked him for the show."

Beckley said that the show would eventually include himself and Sands, as well as UFO historian Allen Greenfield and John Rhodes. Rhodes has had personal experiences with the Men-In-Black and is widely known as a leading authority on reptilian aliens and the unexplained mysteries of the Inner Earth, which is where some researchers think the Men-In-Black may call their home, the netherworlds hidden underground.

"Part of the episode was shot near the Grand Canyon," Beckley said, "and then the UFO Hunters and the crew went on to I think Salt Lake City to shoot the rest of the program. So it probably took about oh, I guess, four or five days to put this all in the can and then several weeks of editing before it is aired nationally. For me, it was a nice trip and an exciting experience, but then again most folks know I love radio, television and filmmaking."

For those unfamiliar with the program, Beckley offered some basic background.

"Each episode of the program involves a different aspect of the UFO phenomenon," he said. "Recently, they've had a show on abductions; they've had a show on the grays; they've had one on undersea saucers or USOs. They've had an episode on pilots who have been buzzed. So each show is themed, and this one is on the Men-In-Black."

Beckley said his interest in the MIB mystery goes back over four decades.

"One of the first books I ever read on UFOs," he recalled, "was by the late Gray Barker and called They *Knew Too Much About Flying Saucers*. In its pages, the author describes how certain UFO researchers had gotten too close to the truth about the origins of and the occupants who pilot the flying discs that were being seen all over America in the 1950s and 60s. The researchers were visited by gentlemen wearing black suits, black hats, sometimes dark sunglasses, usually traveling in black limousines or Cadillacs, who threatened the researchers that if they told what they knew about flying saucers then something tragic would happen to either them or their families.

"Probably the first person to be silenced that we know about," Beckley continued, "is Albert K. Bender, who was the head of the *International Flying Saucer Bureau*, an organization that reigned supreme in the early 1950s. Bender had several thousand members all over the world, and put out a very nice little newsletter called Space Review. And apparently he had printed something he should not have in the pages of his newsletter, which got back to 'them,' whoever they are! We don't know whether they're extraterrestrial. Some of them may be government officials. I have my own theory, which I discuss on the show, as to where the Men-In-Black may be originating."

Bender's tale continued.

"So, these three men appeared at Albert K. Bender's door one day. They proved to him that they were not of earthly or human origin, let's say. They materialized and dematerialized in front of him, and they told him to shut down his international UFO organization, which he did. At around this time, which would have been 1953 or 1954, there were other individuals who were being harassed by these Men-In-Black. There were freaky phone calls and strange poltergeist-like phenomena that were taking place inside the houses of UFO witnesses and heads of various UFO organizations as well."

Beckley told the story of John Stewart, who ran the New Zealand branch of the *International Flying Saucer Bureau* and was attacked by some unknown force and was actually pushed down a flight of stairs in a large department store in front of hundreds of witnesses by some unseen hand. His girlfriend was molested by some invisible creature inside her home. The two were so terrified by what had happened that they immediately quit their UFO investigations, ceased their correspondence and retired from the field, never to be heard from again.

"So little by little," Beckley said, "other researchers started being frightened by these Men-In-Black. This went on for quite a number of years. My work, *UFO Silencers: Mystery of the Men In Black*, detailed many dozens of cases involving these MIBs. And this of course was long before Will Smith and the movie version came out, which was jazzed up for public consumption. There were some pretty strange cases that I wrote about, including one or two incidents where UFO witnesses were savagely attacked and the possible murder of a sixteen-year-old boy found within feet of where a flying saucer had landed on the banks of the New York State Barge Canal in Scotia, on New York's Mohawk River."

But Beckley has done more than simply research the subject of MIBs. He has also had a personal firsthand encounter.

"While I was not the person being stalked or harassed," he said, "I was directly involved in this bizarre incident. There had been a huge flap of sightings up and down the East Coast that lasted from 1965 to 1968. One of the individuals I was associated with, John J. Robinson, had collected a lot of this data. Not just of strange phenomena in the sky, but also of creature sightings, different flying beings, as well as Bigfoot-type apparitions. He was also a researcher into strange events that were taking place underground known as the Shaver Mystery, the Inner Earth mysteries and so forth. He strongly believed that some UFOs might be originating from under our very feet.

"Now Jack, as his friends called him of course, was an associate editor of Jim Moseley's "*Saucer News*." At that time, "*Saucer News*" was the largest UFO publication in the world, with around 12,000 subscribers. Jack wrote articles for Jim's magazine as well as a newsletter I was putting out. Jack lived over in Jersey City but commuted to his day job, which was working at a bank in Manhattan.

"His wife Mary," Beckley went on, "would do the chores and the shopping. Every morning she'd go out around nine o'clock to go to the local supermarket or the deli."

On more than one occasion, Mary reported to Beckley and Moseley, who worked out of an office on Fifth Avenue that served as the "*Saucer News*" headquarters, that whenever she left home she would notice that there was "this strange fellow, almost very, very wooden looking with a very pale face, kind of standing recessed back in a doorway across the street and dressed all in black with a black hat and a black suit on."

The strange interloper appeared to be watching Mary leaving the building as well as watching the activities of other people around her apartment house. Jack and Mary had also been receiving strange phone calls, people calling in the middle of the night and hanging up. Some of their files were broken into and some UFO casebook material disappeared completely.

"So Mary was very, very concerned about this," Beckley said, "and she would call us repeatedly. Well, Jim and I didn't know whether she was just trying to get our attention or whether it was her imagination running wild or whether there really was this individual there stalking the Robinsons. So we decided one morning to take a ride over to Jersey City without letting Mary or Jack know we were coming. We would pay them a surprise visit and see if indeed there was somebody watching their apartment as Mary had insisted."

When Beckley and Moseley arrived, they discreetly passed down the block where the Robinsons lived.

"And sure enough," Beckley recounted, "there was a fellow, just as described, standing in the doorway and peering just off into the distance and dressed in black with a black overcoat, black shoes and black pants. Out in the street, parked right in front of where he was standing, was a black car of some type or another.

"Well, it was fairly early in the morning and it was during rush hour, with very narrow streets, so you couldn't double park or anything. So Jim and I decided to circle the block in Jim's car and see if we couldn't have a conversation with this individual and find out what he was doing standing there on a regular repeat basis. Before pulling away, Jim hands me his camera and I stick it out the window and click the shutter and capture one photo of this 'person' and one of his black vehicle."

After circling the block, which took a full five minutes, the pair returned to find that the stranger and his car were both gone. Beckley feels that the simple act of taking the photo may have scared off the Man-In-Black and the Robinsons never saw or heard from the interloper again.

"So I do believe," Beckley concluded, "that, as far as I know, this is the only authentic photo of what purports to be a true Man-In-Black." Beckley still defends the authenticity of his photo more than forty years later. He told Bill Birnes, Kevin Cook and Patrick Uskert, the three primary characters of the **UFO Hunters** program, that there is no "earthly" reason for the figure to have been standing there at the time or at any other time.

"Several people have suggested, though, that it looked kind of like a pall bearer from a funeral," Beckley said. "Well, I guess you could say it did. Even more peculiar or strange is the fact that once we had confronted this individual by taking a photograph of him, he just sort of slinked into this other realm or other dimension, which is where I believe that the Men-In-Black originate."

And just who or what are the Men-In-Black? Beckley offered more than one theory.

"Some of these individuals may be extraterrestrial," Beckley explained, "because they don't act like humans. They seem to be possessed by a very peculiar behavior pattern. I describe some of the details of these behavior patterns in my book **The UFO Silencers**. Others may be government officials. Still others may be Earth people pulling pranks."

There have been numerous further reports of injuries suffered by witnesses to the Men-In-Black. Beckley recounted the story of a man named Carl Wayne Watts, who had been on his way to meet with the pioneering UFO researcher, the late Dr. J. Allen Hynek.

"Now Mr. Watts had taken several photographs of UFOs," Beckley said, "including a cigar-shaped object hovering in the sky. There was also a picture I used in my book of an alien being who the witness claimed was the occupant of the ship. It looked to me to be some sort of robot with a hard outer shell, or maybe he had a space helmet on. Sort of like the robot in *The Day The Earth Stood Still*. Anyway, on the way to be interviewed by Dr. Hynek, he claimed his automobile was forced off the road and that he was hit over the head by one of these MIBs. After that, course, he refused to talk to anybody, including Dr. Hynek, about his experiences."

Beckley's publishing company, Global Communications, recently released a book called *The Secret Life of Paul Villa*, which also deals in part with harassment by the Men-In-Black.

"Paul Villa was a gentleman of Mexican-American heritage," Beckley said, "who lived in the American Southwest, near Albuquerque, New Mexico, for a good part of his life, which is where he took a series of quite phenomenal UFO photographs from 1962 to around 1973. He says the UFO beings posed their ships especially for him. They can be seen close by in the sky, hovering above his truck, over his house, between trees. Some of them are just within a few feet from the ground. One very remarkable photograph shows an object with tripod landing gear about to land.

"Mr. Villa's story gets pretty wild as he claimed to have had contact with beings from another solar system. He also claims he was harassed by the Men-In-Black as well as by his neighbors. His trailer was set on fire and his truck was overturned. He had to move on several occasions because he felt that his life was in danger and eventually he just kind of disappeared from sight because of this harassment by some unknown force."

Having provided that additional historical background on some of the encounters with the MIB that Beckley has collected over the years, the conversation returned to the recent filming of *UFO Hunters*. Beckley said that over the past forty years he has made several movies himself in addition to working with various motion picture and television production companies, and he can honestly declare that the cast and crew of *UFO Hunters* are a topnotch outfit.

"These fellows had it all together," Beckley said. "A lot of times things were chaotic and hectic and didn't go very smoothly, but the crew there from *UFO Hunters* was very professional and we got the whole thing done on time. Although during the final little segment that I was in, we just caught the last rays of the sun. Another two or three minutes and we would have had to re-shoot the next day. So everything went according to plan. The weather was great and of course the locations out there in Arizona around the Grand Canyon were really fantastic.

"And I must say," he continued, "that of all the crews I've worked with over the years, these guys are really polished and I wouldn't mind working with them again. And of course Bill Birnes is the best. He knows the subject, as did everyone else that was involved with the episode."

There are some critics of the program who fail to give it much in the way of credibility, but Beckley quickly dismissed those negative voices.

"Some people have asked me, well, is everything on *UFO Hunters* for real? Or is it just a lot of hokum and sensationalism? I have to say, regarding the episode that I shot, called **The Silencers**, that everything seemed to be on the up and up. Everyone on the program seemed to be remarkably sure of what they were saying. True, to some, the statements made may be a little more farfetched than people who are into the hardcore science of Ufology, what we call the nuts-and-bolts people, may be comfortable with. They might say, 'Well, there isn't enough evidence.' But these three guys are trying to get to the bottom of the mystery. Nothing is made up on the set; everything is legitimate as far as that goes.

"And I think the **UFO Hunters** do a very good job in getting the information over to the public-a very large percentage of the public who are really not that familiar with the subject whatsoever. You know, it is television, and it has to appeal to a large audience. It's not just what we call 'talking heads.' In order to make a show like this successful, there has to be the appearance of some kind of action. Not just people standing around looking at the sky. For those who find fault with **UFO Hunters**, I strongly recommend they try their hand at producing a UFO-oriented show and see just how easy it is.

"There is room out there for several programs on the subject, but it takes more than talk to produce a series for television. That's 13 shows a season. It's a hump-busting process and one that requires time, dedication, money and of course the ability to sell it to a network.

"But the end result of my involvement with this process," Beckley said, "is that I believe that **UFO Hunters** works within the accepted creative process to present the subject in a fair and balanced manner, without being overly sensationalistic, and represents the best interests of the field. I hope there are future seasons to look forward to."

***More About Tim Beckley***: Involved with the paranormal from an early age, author Timothy Green Beckley has had three UFO sightings. As a teenager, he created one of the first UFO periodicals, which he collated together with mimeographed sheets. Later, he merged his publication with Jim Moseley's "Saucer News." As a journalist, he interviewed John Lennon's girlfriend May Pang, who described Lennon's UFO sighting off his Manhattan terrace of a large circular craft that shot off a beam of light.

Beckley was invited by his late friend, the Earl of Clancarty, Brinsley Le Poer Trench, to speak before a private UFO group formed inside Britain's House of Lords. In addition to his book **The UFO Silencers**, Beckley has authored more than 30 works, including **MJ-12 and the Riddle of Hangar 18, Subterranean Worlds Inside Earth**, and Strange Encounters. For eleven years he edited the nationally distributed **UFO Universe** magazine. Today he writes regularly for Bill and Nancy Birnes at **UFO Magazine** as well as his editorial duties at **www.ConspiracyJournal.com**

This article was originally posted to www.UFODigest.com

## Another Strange Case
## Collected by Robert Goreman

On January 23, 1976, at 5:30 PM, 17-year-old Shirley Greenfield (a pseudonym) was returning home from work and noticed lights cavorting over a reservoir. In seconds, the lights swooped down on her to become a metallic disc directly overhead, possibly thirty feet across and spinning like a top. An invisible force pressed her hard to the ground. Metal fillings in her teeth "vibrated" and a tangy taste filled her mouth. Shirley feared that this unseen "force" would crush her. One half hour of "missing time" was noted when she arrived home, terror-stricken and unable to speak from the shock of the experience.

The event was reported to the police, who refused to investigate and turned the story over to the media. Not seeking publicity, Shirley refused to cooperate with the local press and turned down a lucrative offer for a filmed television interview. Her health had deteriorated and she took to her bed for several days with muscle aches and nausea and vomiting. Her eyes hurt and watered and were quite red. She had unexplained burn marks on her arm and side, as well as a strange purple rash on her neck and shoulders. In her mouth, top dental fillings crumbled into powder and fell out, while some bottom fillings became embedded into the gums.

On Monday, February 2nd, Shirley's mother intercepted a telephone call from a man who would only identify himself as "someone who investigates these things" that asked about her daughter's health and whether any marks had been left on the girl's body as a result of her ordeal. The mother put the caller off.

At 7:00 PM on the following evening, two men arrived at the Greenfield home and demanded "to interrogate" the girl. Both men appeared about 40 and wore crisp black suits and denied being either UFOlogists or journalists. The father initially refused to let them in. One man, tall and fair, almost blond, did all the talking and sternly responded with, "If you do not let us in now, we will come back later and make Shirley speak to us."

Neither man used names. Both had an air of authority and conducted themselves as if they had every right to do and say whatever they chose. The silent partner sat on a chair and held a square black box with no visible moving parts. It was said to be a high-tech recording device. Although this intense grilling session lasted three hours, at no time was any recording tape changed.

The tall one was rude to the point of aggression.

This visit ended with a threat to be silent.

"You must not talk about this matter. It is in your interests not to do so. Nobody will believe you, in any case. In particular, you must not talk to UFO investigators."

The pair left in a large black car.

Mr. Greenfield still wonders, "You know, I have never been able to understand why I did not throw them out. Why I let them hound Shirley for hour after hour. I would normally not tolerate something like this. Why did I let them do this thing?"

The mother was creeped out by the man who had not spoken all night. He continually stared intently at her daughter the entire evening.

These mystery men telephoned the very next day and again a week later. They were still concerned about whether or not the girl had any unusual marks on her body following her ordeal. Shirley finally admitted that, yes, there were marks, but they were gone now. This seemed to satisfy the visitors. They did not contact the family again.

Under the auspices of Dr. Albert Kellar in Manchester, Shirley was hypnotized and asked to relive both the UFO sighting and the visit by the two Men in Black. She reacted in absolute terror to the visit by the MIB and the doctor was forced to abandon the experiment because her vital signs rose to dangerous levels. Even so, Shirley offered a possible clue:

"I don't understand... He's talking to me twice."

This MIB had supposedly interrogated her on two different levels. During the visit, messages had acted upon her subconscious mind in a form of subliminal communication. This advances notions of mental hypnotic suggestion and those Experiments in Distant Influence documented by Dr. Leonid L. Vasiliev.

# MEN IN BLACK...
# REAL LIFE COOKIE MONSTERS!
# BY ATARRC

First Appeared In Your True Tales
September 2003

This true story happened in the summer of 1999. Three friends and I were in an apartment complex made for married couples with children while they attended the University of Northern Iowa. One of my friend's mom was an employee at the school, so she and her sons stayed in the complex with her. Anyway, one July night at midnight we started walking through the complex to the sidewalks that connected with the campus. One of us stopped and pointed to the edge of the sidewalk, which was about 50 feet away. There was this gray-haired man wearing a black silk shirt tucked into khakis pants. He was holding two plastic sacks. Behind him were two men in black cloaks walking in stride together with their hands crossed. My friends and I hustled back over to the corner of last building in the complex where we continued to watch in astonishment as the gray-haired man swung the bags into the woods along the sidewalk. As he turned around, a couple of my friends popped out from the corner. He made eye contact with them, then returned to the woods and grabbed one of the plastic sacks he threw in. He and the two "reapers" walked off toward the front of the complex.

After they walked past, we went to the spot with the sack. My friend Nick, went in to retrieve it. We all huddled around as he pulled out what looked like steering wheel-sized sugar cookies. What the hell?

There are just a lot of unanswered questions, like: What was in the other bag? Why were they throwing sugar cookies in the bushes? What were guys like this doing in a married student housing complex? Why the hell were they dressed in black cloaks... in the middle of July?

# Men In Black Terrorize Witnesses In Calama

The ongoing Chupacabra drama in Calama, a city in northern Chile, took an ominous new twist last week with an appearance by the Men In Black (MIB).

"A resident who saw the alleged Chupacabra was visited and intimidated by odd-looking characters not once but twice, according to Centro UFO de Calama researcher Jaime Ferrer, who conducted field researches of the phenomenon from" March 25 through March 28, 2001.

"The witness and his wife were warned not to speak to Ferrer, whose footsteps are being closely followed by these enigmatic individuals."

"The threatened residents are friends of a third witness to the continuing manifestations and who served as an important source of information.'" to Ferrer.

"Ferrer himself had the following to say: 'On Wednesday night (March 28, 2001) I returned to continue my interview, but my witness behaved oddly and steadfastly refused to talk to me. I didn't know what was going on. I managed to convince him after awhile, and he explained the reason for his attitude."

"The resident, a humble farmer, told him that at 8 o'clock that morning, 'his friend turned up in a truck along with his wife, children, worldly possessions, and the following story.'"

"'Listen, compradito, (Spanish for little friend--J.T.) last night (Tuesday, March 27, 2001) at 11:30 p.m., the three men from the last time turned up at my house . They told us a bunch of stuff. My wife heard it all, and we are in a heap of trouble. Something very bad is going on, and we have to be careful. They mentioned the name of one Jaime Ferrer, the guy who researches and makes plaster casts of things and they said it (Jaime's investigation--J.T.) will lead nowhere. They said you are giving him information about them. I don't know what's going on here, but I'm leaving and I can't stay any longer.'"

"Ferrer said that he had 'in fact discovered and copied several (Chupacabra) prints the previous day.'"

"That evening, myself and others who were with me clearly heard the long, braying sound of the Chupacabra--no other animal can contain such a sound for over 40 seconds."

"Far from being intimidated by the MIBs, Ferrer said he will continue to pursue his research." (See the Chilean newspaper La Estrella del Loa for April 26, 2001, "Chupacabra researcher in the crosshairs of the Men In Black." Muchas gracias a Scott Corrales y Jaime Ferrer para eso articulo de diario.)

Credit - UFO Round Up

# MOTHMEN AND MEN IN BLACK

original source unknown : fair use notice

What may well have been the most notorious of all "scares" involving reptilian beings, involved a combined "invasion" of pterodactylin-hominoid "Mothmen" and "Men In Black". These creatures have been referred to as Mothmen, Winged Dracos, and Winged Serpents, depending on the source involved. They reportedly terrorized a particular area in West Virginia, according to John A. Keel, in the mid-1960's. Keel is convinced that these malevolent entities were involved in the tragic "silver bridge" disaster in which several UFO witnesses perished, based on certain strange circumstances surrounding the event. In his own unique journalistic style Keel reveals the following:

"The moment I met Mary. Hyre's niece Connie Carpenter in 1966, I knew she was telling the truth because her eyes were reddened, watery, and almost swollen shut. I had seen these symptoms many times in my treks around the country investigating UFO reports. Witnesses who were unlucky enough to have a close encounter with an unidentified flying object, usually a dazzlingly brilliant aerial light, are exposed to actinic rays...ultraviolet rays...which can cause 'eye burn,' medically known as KLIEG CONJUNCTIVITIS. These are the same kind of rays that tan your hide at the beach. If you lie in the bright sun without protecting your eyes you can get conjunctivitis. Whatever they are, UFOs radiate intense actinic rays. There are now thousands of cases in which witnesses suffered eye-burns and temporary eye damage...even temporary blindness...after viewing a strange flying light in the night sky.

"...What puzzled me about Connie's case, however, was that she had not seen a splendid luminous flying saucer. She had seen a giant 'winged man' in broad daylight.

"According to her story, Connie, a shy, sensitive eighteen- year-old, was driving home from church at 10:30 A.M. on Sunday, November 27, 1966, when, as she passed the deserted greens of Mason County Golf Course outside New Haven, West Virginia, she suddenly saw a huge gray figure. It was shaped like a man, she said, but much larger. It was at least SEVEN FEET TALL and very broad. The thing that attracted her attention was not its size but its eyes. IT HAD, SHE SAID, LARGE, ROUND, FIERCELY GLOWING RED EYES THAT FOCUSED ON HER WITH HYPNOTIC EFFECT.

"'It's a wonder I didn't run off the road and have a wreck,' she commented later.

"As she slowed, her eyes fixed on the apparition, a pair of wings unfolded from its back. They seemed to have a span of about ten feet. It was definitely not an ordinary bird but a MAN-SHAPED THING which rose slowly off the ground, straight up like a helicopter, silently. Its wings did not flap in flight. It headed straight toward

Connie's car, its horrible eyes fixed to her face, then it swooped low over her head as she shoved the accelerator to the floor-boards in utter hysteria.

"OVER ONE HUNDRED PEOPLE WOULD SEE THIS BIZARRE CREATURE THAT WINTER.

"Connie's conjunctivitis lasted over two weeks, apparently caused by those glowing red eyes. At the time of my first visit to Point Pleasant in 1966 I did not relate the winged weirdo to flying saucers. Later events not only proved that a relationship existed, but that relationship also is a vital clue to the whole mystery.

"Max's Kansas City is a famous watering hole for New York's hip crowd. In the summer of 1967 an oddball character wandered into that restaurant noted for its oddball clientele. He was tall and awkward, dressed in an ill-fitting black suit that seemed out of style. His chin came to a sharp point and his eyes bulged slightly like 'thyroid eyes.' He sat down in a booth and gestured to the waitress with his long, tapering fingers.

"'Something to eat,' he mumbled. The waitress handed him a menu. He stared at it uncomprehendingly, apparently unable to read. 'Food,' he said almost pleadingly.

"'How about a steak?' she offered.

"'Good.'

"She brought him a steak with all the trimmings. He stared at it for a long moment and then picked up his knife and fork, glancing around at the other diners. It was obvious he did not know how to handle the implements! The waitress watched him as he fumbled helplessly. Finally she showed him how to cut the steak and spear it with the fork. He sawed away at the meat. Clearly he really was hungry.

"'Where are you from?' she asked gently.

"'Not from here.'

"'Where?'

"'Another world.'

"Boy, another put-on artist, she thought to herself. The other waitresses gathered in a corner and watched him as he fumbled with his food, a stranger in a strange land.

"A large white car with a faulty muffler wheezed and rattled up the back street in New Haven, West Virginia, where Connie Carpenter lived, and Jack Brown knocked at her door.

"'I'm a--a friend of Mary Hyre's.'

"His strange demeanor and disjointed questions distressed her and disturbed her husband, Keith, and her brother Larry. It quickly became obvious that he was not particularly interested in Connie's sighting of the man-bird the year before. He seemed more concerned with Mrs. Hyre and my own relationship with her (we were professional friends, nothing more).

"'What do you think--if--what would Mary Hyre do--if someone told her to stop writing about UFOs?' he asked.

"'She'd probably tell them to drop dead.' Connie replied.

"Most of the questions were stupid, even unintelligible.

After a rambling conversation he drove off into the night in his noisy car. Connie called her aunt immediately, puzzled and upset by the visit. He was such a very odd man, she noted, and he wouldn't speak at all if you weren't looking directly into his dark, hypnotic eyes. Connie, Keith and Larry not only noticed his long-fingered hands, but there was also something very peculiar about his ears. They couldn't say exactly what. But there was something...

"Another kind of Man in Black haunted Brooklyn, New York, in 1877-80. He had wings and performed aerial acrobatics over the heads of the crowds of sunbathers at Coney Island. A Mr. W. H. Smith first reported these strange flights in a letter to the NEW YORK SUN, September 18, 1877. The creature was not a bird, but a 'winged human(oid) form.'

"This flying 'man' became a local sensation and, according to the NEW YORK TIMES, September 12, 1880, 'many reputable persons' saw him as he was 'engaged in flying toward New Jersey.' He maneuvered at an altitude of about one thousand feet, sporting 'BATS WINGS' and making swimming like movements. Witnesses claimed to have seen his face clearly. He 'WORE A CRUEL AND DETERMINED EXPRESSION.' The entire figure was black, standing out sharply against the clear blue sky...

"North American Indians have extensive legends about the Thunderbird, a huge bird said to carry off children and old people. It was accompanied by loud noises, hums, buzzes and, apparently rumbles from the infrasonic and ultrasonic levels. Known as PIASA to the Indians of the Dakotas, it was supposed to have terrifying red eyes and a long tail... a monstrous demon with... bat's wings, and a body closely in human form.

"...In May 1961, a New York pilot was buzzed by a 'damned big bird, bigger than an eagle. For a moment I doubted my sanity because it looked more like a pterodactyl out of the prehistoric past.' The thing had swooped at his plane as he cruised up the Hudson River valley.

"Far away, in the Ohio River valley, another startled pair had an even more breathtaking experience. A woman prominent in civic affairs in Point Pleasant, West Virginia, was driving on Route 2 along the Ohio River with her elderly father. As they passed through a sector on the edge of the park known as the Chief Cornstalk Hunting Grounds, a tall manlike figure suddenly appeared on the road in front of them.

"'I slowed down,' she told me years later, 'and as we got closer we could see that it was much larger than a man. A big gray figure. It stood in the middle of the road. Then a pair of wings unfolded from its back and they practically filled the whole road. It almost looked like a small airplane. Then it took off straight up...disappeared out of sight in seconds. We were both terrified. I stepped on the gas and raced out of there.

"...A businessman in Arlington, Virginia, wrote to me recently, describing an experience he and three friends had in the winter of 1969-69. They were at a farm near Haymarket when they heard a strange rushing sound near a small lake. Intrigued, they set out with flashlights and a couple of dogs to investigate. Suddenly the dogs howled, turned tail, and ran.

There, standing by a tree was a huge dark shadow between eight and twelve feet tall. The quartet scurried back to their car, turned on their lights, and swung toward the shadow. 'All we saw,' he reported, 'was this huge thing with large red-orange eyeballs and winglike arms. We couldn't get out of there fast enough.'"

Keel goes on to relate the experience of Woodrow Derenberger, who experienced a weird encounter on November 4th (1966?) while driving on Route 7 outside of Parkersburg "when he suddenly felt a tingling sensation in his forehead." Then thoughts from a being that identified itself as Indrid Cold from the planet 'Lanulos' "began to spring full-blown in his mind." According to Keel:

"Two weeks later, though Woody wasn't aware of it at the time, two salesmen visited Mineral Wells and went from house to house with their wares. They weren't very interested in making sales. At one house they offered bibles. At another, hardware. At a third they were 'Mormon missionaries from Salem, Oregon' (a UFO wave was taking place in Salem at that time). One man was tall, blond, and looked like a Scandinavian. His partner was short and slight, with pointed features and a dark olive complexion. They asked questions about Woody and were particularly interested in opinions on the validity of his alleged contact..."

were sold to the Trojan-U.S. Powder Co. and the LFC Chemical Co. Some were leased to American Cyanamid.

\* \* \* \* \*

John Keel personally investigated the TNT area and claimed that in one area an irrational "fear" gripped him. He would step out of the large circle and the sensation would cease. He again entered it and soon the induced atmosphere of fear and terror would almost overcome him until he was forced to leave it. Could this have been the site of an underground lair?

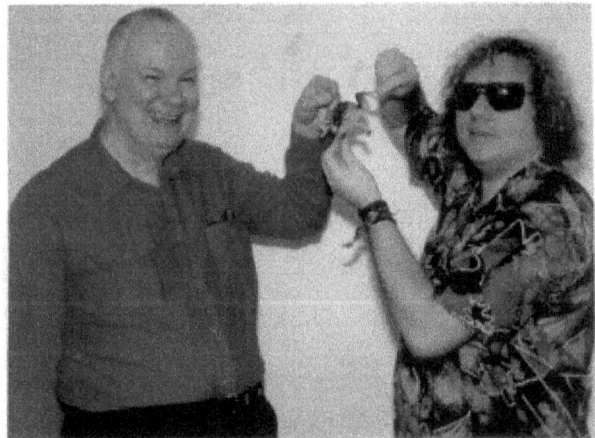

John - "*Mothman Prophecies*" - Keel presents Inner Light's Tim Beckley with the FOrtean Society Of The Year Award, its mascot pet (rubber) frog. Keel has long written about his occult experiences in the Far East. Frogs represent the strange fall -- or "teleportation" of mysterious objects from the sky as first described by historian Charles Fort (thus the term "Fortean")

Remember, the entire area is honeycombed with tunnels which have for years been sealed off to the public. Keel related other accounts of encounters where witnesses saw these pterodactylin 'mothmen', one of which entered one of the old buildings that led to the tunnels. Investigators followed the creature into the dome but the winged reptile seemed to have vanished. Keel related other incident involving the dreaded MIB. Referring to the investigations of a fellow researcher by the name of Dan Drisin, he reveals:

"...During his second visit to Point Pleasant Dan uncovered some Mothmen witnesses I had missed. And he also came across some more baffling Men-In-Black-type reports. People up in the back hills has been seeing mysterious unmarked panel trucks which sometimes parked for hours in remote spots. There seemed to be several of these trucks in the area and the rumor was that they belonged to the air force. Men in neat coveralls were seen monkeying with telephone and power lines but no one questioned them.

"A woman living alone on an isolated island north of Vancouver, British Columbia, Canada, had two curious encounters with the same kind of beings. She had moved to a tiny one-room cabin on Keats Island in October 1967 and was soon seeing UFO lights nightly. On January 29, 1968, following a close sighting of 'a long dark body with dim red and yellow lights at both ends,' she was surprised by two visitors. Both wore 'neat, dark coveralls' and claimed to be employees of the hydroelectric company. They offered to help her put up a stovepipe. The younger of the two climbed on the roof of her cabin while the other handed him the pipes. 'I could hear the man on the ground directing him and the one on the roof would answer, "Yes, Master".'

"After the pipe was installed, the pair joined her for tea. They seemed 'a little stiff.' When they left she wondered how they had known she was there because 'the cabin couldn't be seen from the road (and) the stove was out when they arrived, so there was no smoke from the chimney.'

"On May 2, she again encountered two men. 'One was the 'boss' Hydro man in his neat coveralls,' she reported (CANADIAN UFO REPORT, #13, 1972-73). 'The other was different, younger and about 19-20. As I entered the path, the boss man indicated with his hand for the young man to get behind him. They got well off the path and waited for me, the young man a little behind his boss. The fellow stared at me as if I were some kind of freak...'

"This time she didn't invite them for tea. One odd thing she noticed during both meetings was their slow, careful way of walking. They looked at their feet and stepped uncertainly. "The next day a jeep came along the road, containing four men inspecting lines... 'carelessly dressed, workaday men, none in coveralls. The boss wasn't obviously so. They expressed no surprise at seeing me there, no concern or any particular interest. I told them two of their men had already been around the day before, inspecting the lines. They assured me yesterday's men weren't Hydro men, that somebody had been "pulling my leg."'

"Somebody was also pulling a lot of legs in cosmopolitan Long Island. In West Virginia I had heard some stories about three men who looked 'like Indians' and were accompanied by a fourth man, more normal-looking and very shabbily dressed in contrast to the other three. So I was nonplused when I heard identical descriptions from people on Long Island.

"An elderly woman who lived alone in a house near the summit of Mount Misery, the highest point on Long Island, had received a visit from this quartet in early April 1967, immediately after a severe rainstorm.

"'They had high cheekbones and very red faces, like a bad sunburn,' she told

me. 'They were very polite but they said my land belonged to their tribe and they were going to get it back. What frightened me was their feet. They didn't have a car...they must have walked up that muddy hill...but their shoes were spotlessly clean. There was no trace of mud or water where they walked in my house.'

"That same week another visitor came to Mount Misery. This was a woman with striking white hair who claimed to represent a local newspaper. She carried a book 'like a big ledger' and asked the witness a number of personal questions about her family background. When I later checked with the newspaper I found they employed no one of that description.

"The local Mount Misery expert was Miss Jane P. Paro, a radio personality then with station WBAB in Babylon, New York. Miss Paro is a dark-haired, dark-eyed young lady with a soft, haunting voice. At that time she conducted an interview show, largely devoted to the historical psychic lore of the region. Soon after she reported some UFO sightings around Mount Misery she began to receive all manner of crank calls, both at the station and on her UNLISTED home phone. METALLIC VOICES ordered her to meet them on 'the Mount' (she didn't go).

"...Mount Misery is a heavily wooded hill with a few narrow dirt roads slicing through it and a number of large mansions set back among the trees. The late Henry Stimson, secretary of war during World War II, maintained a lavish estate on the summit. For decades the Mount was known as a haunted place, THE SITE OF A NUMBER OF MYSTERIOUS DEATHS AND DISAPPEARANCES. In the spring of 1967, young couples necking on the back roads began to see low- flying UFOs, particularly around a field that was used as a junkyard for old cars. Others claimed to see a giant hairy monster with gleaming red eyes..."

# THEY'VE COME TO TAKE YOU AWAY

The state of Arizona has always been a hotbed (pardon the expression) of UFO activity. Maybe it has something to do with Wendelle Stevens living there (only kidding Wendelle), but nevertheless I can remember a handful of MIB reports being handed to me.

Take for example the case of a Tucson newsboy, Warren Weisman who was delivering the *Daily Star* on Feb 19, 1979 at around 6 AM when he saw an odd looking object crash into a parked car at the side of the road.

According to a newspaper account this is his story:

"I was on Winstel Blvd when I saw this 'falling star' come from the sky. It was traveling at great speed and landed about a block away. It smashed the back of a white Volkswagen, throwing off its right rear wheel, rolled off the car and knocked over a mailbox on a post nearby."

The ten year old fifth grader said the object was about the size of a microwave oven, was black, shiny, and had lots of "lava-like" holes all around it. Weisman said the object was smoking when he walked over to it.

As he bent over to examine his unusual find a brown pulled up and says the witness, "A skinny man in a brown suit and white shirt got out of the car. He was an FBI-type. He told me, "Why don't you go ahead and deliver the rest of the papers?"

As he stood talking to the man, what Warren thinks was a Pima County Sheriff's car pulled up along side the brown car. "I was afraid that the man in the brown suit was going to pull a gun," Warren said. He quickly departed from home to tell his mother about what had happened.

Twenty minutes later, he returned to the scene of the "crash" with his mother.

"All we found was the tire and the broken mailbox." The smashed car and the smoking object had totally vanished without a trace.

Interviewed later, the boy claimed he had put a small chip from the object into his pocket while looking it over. However, when he got hom a little while later it was gone.

"I don't know what happened to it," he confessed. "I didn't  have any holes in my pocket from which it could have fallen to the ground."

What at first might seem to be a tale story  fabricated by a highly imaginative youth has additional verification in that there were other witnesses to the event.

The *Arizona Daily Star* says that "three counselors who patrol the area while children deliver newspapers saw it fall but didn't see where it hat the ground."

The woman who lives in the house where the mailbox was knocked down, said she and her family assumed someone had hit it with a car. Margaret Pierce said she hadn't heard anything unusual that morning, but around the time Warren usually delivers the paper to their house "our dogs just started barking and we couldn't calm them down. They were really upset and that's not like them at all."

At the time the UFO group APRO was still active in Tucson and were called upon to make an investigation. As far as is known they never issued a report, and in the meanwhile Warren Weisman remained one frightened individual due to a possible visit by an MIB.

# Men In Black In Phoenix

Take for example this report that was posted on the website of the UFO Clearing House. . .


**Phoenix, Arizona Men In Black Encounter**
**Posted on December 20, 2009 at 7:17 PM**
**Case Number: 21068**
**Log Number: US-12202009-0007**
**Submitted Date: 2009-12-20 16:21 GMT**
**Event Date: 1988-02-15 21:00 GMT**
**Status: Assigned**
**City: PHOENIX**
**Region: Arizona**
**Country: US**
**Longitude: -112.081**
**Latitude: 33.4979**
**Shape: Disc**


Around 1989 I was working at a restaurant in Scottsdale, Az. I was speaking with a customer and somehow we were on the subject of life on other planets. I recall saying something to the effect of "The odds are that there has to be life on other planets, due to the vast number of planets". Another customer overheard me say this and said "Do you really believe that"? I said "Yes, I do". He said "Next time I come in, I am going to show you something". He had a serious demeanor as he said this. I had no idea what to expect. A few days later he came in and had a brief case with him. This brief case was totally dedicated to this UFO encounter he had experienced. He showed me a map of Arizona, where he had outlined the area that he had encountered a UFO in. It was the Roosevelt Lake area, north of Phoenix. He then pulled out a Polaroid photo he had taken. .

I stared at that photo for 20 minutes. It is THE most realistic photo of a UFO I have ever seen. And it was VERY close up. The photo was taken from about 50 ft. away. It was taken at night and the ONLY light source was from the UFO itself! It was so apparent that I didn't even ask if he had used a flash. I was obvious he had not, so I just said, unassumingly, "Why didn't you use a flash"? His eyes got huge, and he said "Are you kidding! They would have seen me". The reason you could tell the light was emanating from the craft was because the foliage to the left on the image was illuminated from behind. The foliage was in front of the craft, from the vantage point of the camera. The leaves were black, not green, as would be expected if the light source were from the camera. You could see only the outline of the foliage, not detail, as one would see from a camera flash.

The craft was the classic disc-shaped kind. It was gray and metallic looking. The lower portion of the craft was concealed, due to a cliff overhang that it was hovering behind. I would gauge the craft to be about 60 ft. from side to side. The craft was about 50-60 ft. away from the camera-taker. The most fascinating part on the craft was the light on it. There was an orb, about the size of a basketball, that was circling the middle, most wide part of the craft. The orb was pure white in color, with not a tinge of yellow or blue. The reason you could tell the orb was circling the craft was due to the fact that the camera had captured a tail trailing the orb, as would a tail on a comet. So I tell they guy, after freaking out on the amazing authenticity of his photo, that he has to show this to someone. He said "I plan to. There is a professor/ufologist at ASU that is interested in this". So I see the guy several days later and he said he had taken the photo to the ASU (Arizona State University) guy. He said the ASU professor also said it was the best UFO photo he had ever seen. I see the guy several days later, again, and ask him what the ASU professor guy is doing with the photo and such. He starts acting really weird. He wouldn't answer me. I asked him again. His demeanor was that he was pissed off.

He said to me "I'm not allowed to talk about it". I said "What? What do you mean?" He said "I'm not allowed to talk about it". He is really agitated. I can't resist, so I said "Oh come on". He said "I'm not allowed to talk about it. Two men from the government showed up at my door and said I am not allowed to mention this again, or I will disappear. They took the photo from the ASU professor and threatened him as well". Since then I have read much info on UFO phenomena. Interestingly, much of what I have read about MIB, is that they appear at someone's door, as a pair of two men, to threaten the experiencer. Mind you, his experience was long before MIB, the movie, came out, and MIB became part of general consciousness. I had never heard of MIB at this point.

The internet had not taken off yet, so he didn't research the MIB phenomena to add credence to his story. He didn't need to anyway, with that photo! It now makes sense to me that these government guys take only the good photos, and leave the junk out there. Thus when the general public views the photos, they assume the whole phenomena is people's imaginations, or pranks. They purposely allow the crappy photos to prevail. If anyone knows who the ASU professor may have been, could you please contact a MUFON representative. I cannot imagine there were many ASU professors/ufologists at the time

# MIB and A Black Helicopter

**Monday, February 08, 2010**
**Alien Contact / MIB - Tonopah, Arizona**
**Tonopah, Arizona - July 1, 2009 - 10:30 PM (report unedited):**

While in the desert near the Palo Verde Nuclear Plant, the main witness and some friends saw a very large triangle shaped UFO. They were driving down a dirt road and saw a bright flashing light. They had seen objects in the area before and their intentions were to look for UFO's. According to the witnesses, people that live in this area have been chased in their cars and seen objects on a regular basis. They went off the road behind some mountains, and no sooner had they come around the mountain they saw the large flashing light. All of them were scared but, at the same time, curious.

The main witness friend's girlfriend was crying and telling them to turn around; they got within 2 to 300 yards from the light. It was the size of three football fields, triangular in shape, and had windows around it. It was about 3 stories tall, and about 30 feet off the ground, they flashed their lights and it flashed back, in the same sequence of flashes. The main witness and his friend, James, got out of the car and walked closer. The closer they got, the better they could make out what was standing in the windows. They could see small big headed aliens, and then 7 to 9 foot tall aliens, they based this on the size of the windows. Some of the windows they could see through, the other windows were dark, but then the dark windows, cleared up one by one, and as they went clear more and more aliens appeared on the windows. James was supposedly videotaping the whole time. The main witness was terrified but excited at the same time.

They walked closer and had to stop because the heat coming from the craft was so intense. The craft hovered and then landed. A large panel at the bottom of the craft opened and two aliens proceeded to walk out. This absolutely terrified the witnesses, but they couldn't move or talk. The main witness remembers trying to scream and run but they couldn't move or talk. Two others were in the car honking the horn, and screaming for them to come back, but they couldn't respond or move.

The aliens walked up to within 20 feet of them. One of them was very thin and tall, about 8-9 feet, the other one was about 3-4 feet tall. The witnesses stood there in amazement, shocked because they couldn't move or speak. Then calmness came over them and the aliens began speaking to them telepathically, they were saying not to be scared that they were not going to harm them. This "conversation" went on between the 4 of them for 15-20 minutes. They said they were here to help us, so that we would not destroy our planet, and that there was a horrible event coming soon, that it had to be stopped. One of the witnesses asked if it was something like '9/11' and they said that it was bigger and that it would come from the Middle East. The main witness then thought to himself that he had been in this situation before and the tall alien heard his thoughts and repeated his name and said that yes, he had been visited before when he was 6 years old in Deming, New Mexico. He had been in the desert exploring and they had talked to him then. He had blocked that out, but it all suddenly came back, they said they knew they were coming and wanted them to warn people about global warming and what was to come if they didn't take start taking care of our planet. Visions of disaster then entered their heads, as if to show them what was to come.

The taller alien then walked closer, and held his hand. He was no longer scared, neither was his friend, James. They said that they would see them again soon and to warn people about 'saving our planet'. Supposedly James was recording the whole time. The aliens then returned to the craft and it was gone in a split second. When the craft left they both felt weak, but managed to make their way back to the car, when they got there the occupants of the car, Heather and Jamie, were not crying anymore they just hugged the witnesses.

For a minute the car would not start and suddenly it just turned on by itself. As they started to drive away three military helicopters appeared and began shining their lights on the witnesses. Then two military Hummers showed up and chased the witnesses. They tried to avoid the Hummers but were told over a speaker to pull over or they would be forced to shoot at them. They pulled over and military personnel surrounded their vehicle.

Two men dressed in black opened the door and asked them to get out. One of them looked familiar to the main witness. He asked the witnesses to get out and both questioned them, while the military personnel searched the car. They asked them what they had seen, how long they had been there and if they had had any contact with the alien ship. One of the soldiers then found the video camera. The men in black reviewed it and told the witnesses they were not to speak of this, they then confiscated the camera and took the main witness with them. The other 3 witnesses asked where they were going and they told them not to worry about it. He left with them and they questioned him further. He kept staring at one of the men since he looked familiar. They then dropped him off on the I-10 highway near Tonopah Joe's restaurant. There he was later picked up by his friends.

Source: NUFORC

NOTE: this area is in western Maricopa County, Arizona, approximately 50 miles west of downtown Phoenix off Interstate 10. The community of Tonopah is near the Palo Verde Nuclear Generating Station, the largest nuclear power plant in the country. There have been considerable UFO/alien accounts from this general area including rumors that an underground facility is nearby...Lon

May of those who have been harassed by the Men in Black claim they were later set upon by mysterious black helicopters like in this illustration by Carol Ann Rodriguez.

# MIBS, UFOS, AND THE CARLOS ALLENDE LETTERS

Ever since organized flying saucer research began in the early 1950's a disturbing number of serious UFO investigators have suffered personal harassment, unusual accidents and even mysterious deaths. In some cases, sinister voices have whispered threats over the telephone and warned certain researchers to terminate specific investigations. Recently an increasing number of civilian UFOlogists have been visited by ominous strangers who have made it physically clear that their orders to discontinue all UFO investigations would be violently enforced. Official disclaimers have only served to intensify the mystery of the bizarre incidents currently seeding chaos within the rank of civilian UFO investigators and instilling fear among those who witness flying-saucer activity.

It was in September 1953, that three agents of a silence group made their first in-person visit. Albert K. Bender, who had organized an international flying-saucer bureau, was their target.

Allende claims he was witness to the Philadelphia Experiment tied in with the death of Dr. M.K. Jessup.

According to ufologist Gray Barker, Bender had received certain data which he felt provided the missing pieces for a theory concerning the origin of flying saucers. Bender wrote down his thesis and sent it off to a friend he felt he could trust. When the three men appeared at Benders door, one of them held that letter in his hand.

The three men told Bender that among the many saucer researchers he had been the one to stumble upon the correct answer to the flying saucer enigma. Then they filled him in on the details. Bender became ill. He was unable to eat for three days.

UFO investigators Dominick Lucchesi and August C. Roberts called on Bender and encouraged him to break his silence concerning the mysterious men in black.

"They were pretty rough with me," Bender told them, "Two men did all the talking and the other kept watching me all the time they were here. He didn't take his eyes off me."

Bender went on to say that when people found out the truth about flying saucers there would be dramatic changes in all things. Science, especially would suffer a major blow. Political structures would topple. Mass confusion would reign. Roberts and Lucchesi kept chipping away at Benders wall of silence, but to most of their queries they received only a noncommittal "I cannot answer that".

A middle aged Albert K. Bender seldom tackled the subject of UFOs after he says he was silenced by the MIB.

In 1962, Bender declared that he would at last tell his story to the world in "Flying Saucers and the Three Men". This perplexing volume served only to confuse serious researchers, as it told of Benders astral projection to a secret underground saucer base in Antarctica that was manned by male, female and bisexual creatures. The question which remained to plague UFO investigators were many. Were Benders experiences really of a psychic nature? Was his book deliberately contrived to hide the true nature of his silencing? Had the whole experience been clothed in an extended metaphor that might yield certain clues to the perspective researcher?

On June 24, 1967, Dominick Lucchesi told the authors that Bender seemed to be a changed man after the three man in black had visited him. "It was as if he had been lobotomized," Lucchesi said. "He was scared and later he suffered from tremendous headaches which he said were controlled 'them!' Whenever he would think about breaking his silence, one of his terrific headaches would just about knock him out."

"The three men shut him up and he stayed shut-up," August Roberts added. "Today Bender manages a motel in California. We still correspond, but he still refuses to discuss flying saucers."

"In my opinion," Lucchesi said, "the men in black are representatives of an organization on this planet, but they are not from any known bureau in our government. I believe both these men and the UFO'S come from some civilization which has flourished in a remote area of the Earth, such as the Amazon, the North Gobi Desert, or the Himalaya Mountains. It is possible that these are underground civilizations."

Within a few months after Bender had been silenced, John H. Stuart, a New Zealander, picked up a piece of metal that had fallen from a UFO during a close sighting in February, 1955. The next night he received a visit from a men dressed in black who announced that he had more right than Stuart did to the piece of grey-white metal. The man in black told Stuart a lot about flying- saucers, "...too much, maybe,

Though they often arrive as a trio there is just as likely to be one of them standing by their ominous black vehicle.

for my own personal safety," Stuart wrote Gray Barker.

"It is easy to understand why they told me what they did, it was meant to scare the hell out of me, - it did! I had plenty of fright in the last world war and I am the first to admit I was very scared after this 'gentleman' had left."

Some researchers feel that certain of their fellows may have ignored the threats of the silencers and paid the ultimate price for their bravery.

Astrophysicist Morris K. Jessup, who had been vitally interested in UFO research, received an unusual series of letters concerning UFO'S, secret Navy experiments, disappearing ships, and invisible men, from a mysterious correspondent who signed himself as Carlos Allende.

Another member of Benders International Flying Saucer Bureau was the late August C Roberts who had taken several UFO photographs thought to be legitimate. Roberts was later to be drawn into the mystery of the Men In Black because of his association with Bender. Here he is seen interviewing George Stock who took a close up snap shot of a flying saucer near Jersey City.

The letters, postmarked from Texas and Pennsylvania, seemed important enough to the Office of Naval Research to form a special study group assigned to ferret out the mystery. Although official investigation seemed to bog down, Jessup pursued his independent research into the flying-saucer puzzle. The astrophysicist subsequently was found dead in his automobile outside a park in Florida, an alleged suicide.

In the late 1940s, Ray Palmer founded FATE magazine with Curt Fuller gave the UFO enigma its first big publicity push. The Air Force dubbed Palmer the "Father of Flying Saucers" and accused the editor-publisher of having fabricated the whole business to boost sales of his magazine. "I only wish I was that smart." said Palmer in 1967.

Today Ray Palmer edits Flying Saucers, Search and Space World from a small but impressive publishing company in Amherst, Wisconsin. Palmer is one researcher who has been involved in the UFO mystery from the beginning. In June 1947, Palmer sent businessman- pilot Kenneth Arnold, who "discovered" flying saucers, to Tacoma, Washington. There, Arnold became embroiled in the famous Mairy Island incident which, according to Palmer "ended in terror and disaster and the deaths of two fine Fourth Air Force secret-service officers"

The Maury Island affair was quickly written off as a hoax by Air Force investigators, but a cautious examination of Arnolds testimony indicates that there is a mystery inherent in the incident which cannot yet be solved. For one thing, the cast of characters for the strange drama includes at least two nearly omniscient men in black who antedate Benders visitors by six years.

Palmers name is also linked to Richard Shaver's bizarre "memories" of Lemuria, a cave world, Dero, rays, contrived train wrecks, mental control and ancient space ships.

If you ask Ray Palmers opinion about MIB (men in black), he will tell you that he considers the whole business a myth, a fiction.

"I have been visited by every governmental intelligence agency in existence," Palmer said, "and have all presented proper credentials. I have never been visited by any MIBs or by anyone who threatened me. And if anyone should be a target for these visits, it should be me!"

"But what about the dero?" he was reminded. "In an issue of Search wrote that the dero (evil cave-culture aliens) once nearly got your life, that you live of perpetual and terrible pain, that never subsides for a second. You also wrote: 'I KNOW the dero are real, and I KNOW what they can do!'"

Palmer did not avoid the question, but he phrased his answer cautiously. "First of all, let me say that there is certainly something to the flying saucer mystery. But where do UFO'S come from? That's like asking where do we go when we die? There is no one answer and there is no easy answer and maybe several people have different answers and maybe they're all right! I think there are strong link-ups with psychism in the UFO mystery. I feel there is a great deal of psychic deception going on. But WHO is practising such deception - that is the problem!"

"My experience with the dero took place when I was still editing FATE in Evanston, Illinios. One night we had a very hard rainstorm and the drain in the basement plugged up. I was wading around in the water, trying to unstop the drain, when I suddenly felt myself being lifted high into the air. Helpless, I hung suspended for just a moment, then I was slammed down to the basement floor with great force. I was paralysed as a result of this attack and I most certainly do bear the effects of this paralysis to this day. I am not certain WHAT attacked me, but I am certain it was no accident."

In an "Open Letter to all UFO Researchers," which was published in an issue of SAUCER SCOOP, John Keel set forth his opinion that the MIBs are the intelligence arm of a large and possibly hostile group. After discussing various type of contact, Keel went on to say that he considered the MIBs to be professional terrorists ..." and among their many duties is the harassment of the UFO researchers who become too involved in cases which might reveal too much of the truth."

Keel's pursuit of the silencers has led him to uncover some extreme cases of personal abuse in which certain contactee's or investigators have been kidnapped by three MIBs in a black car. The researcher notes that "it is nearly always THREE men" who subject the victim to some sort of brain - washing technique that leaves him in a state of nausea, mental confusion, or even amnesia lasting for several days. "All such victims have a black eye when released," Keel writes, "which suggests that physical contact of a violent nature is a necessary part of the brainwashing treatment."

Keels "Open Letter" in SAUCER SCOOP concludes with words of admonition and warning:

"We are now on a vicious merry-go-round and we are caught in the middle of this bizarre conflict. Contacts are being made... then suppressed... on a dizzying scale. Information is being gained... then lost... at an ever increasing pace. One of the ironies of all this is that no policeman in his right mind associates black cars, kidnappers, amnesia victims and black eyes with the UFO phenomena. Many of these cases never got beyond local police departments. Neither the FBI nor any other central government agency is engaged in collecting information on these aspects. Even local newspapers seldom take notice of these cases... since the victims are often children and teenagers... most newspapers make an effort to protect young people by suppressing "crime news" involving them.

"Because the official law-enforcement agencies are unwilling, or unable, to cope with this ever-growing situation, it becomes the responsibility of the private civilian investigator to collect and collate the full details on these incidents. The hazards of such investigations are obvious, but the job must be done. And it must be done fast, with courage and intelligence."

"All of this has been brought upon us because we have wasted years chasing lights in the sky and fussing with the Air Force. We have allowed a serious volatile situation to develop under our noses while we played with aimless speculations about the origin and nature of those rather insignificant vehicles overhead. We must switch our attention from the vehicles to the occupants. The menace is not in our skies. It is on the ground and is at this moment spreading like a disease across the country and the world."

*Albert K. Bender's Sketch of a Man in Black*

One of the Bender memorabilia, this is a drawing of what the UFO researcher says one of the MIB looked like.

In his address to the 1967 Congress of Scientific UFOlogists, Keel told of his personal mission to track down the silencers. He said that dark-completed mystery men had some times silenced saucer sightings BEFORE the witnesses had time to report the sighting. On occasion, Keel said, he has arrived on the scene within moments after the mysterious silencers had departed.

According to Keel, the MIBs visited and silenced eight whole communities in Washington in May 1967. Several homes in Long Island were unwilling hosts to the silencers in June. Keel also noted a large number of dog kidnappings occurring at the time the MIBs were calling upon saucer sighters.

"The UFO'S don't want us to know where they are from," Keel stated. "They have been lying to contactee's since 1897!" (Keel explained this reference by stating that the first man in black may have appeared in Texas in 1897 when, according to newspaper accounts, some "pottery" had fallen from a mysterious airship. The next day, a dark-suited man of "Oriental complexion" arrived in town and bought up the strange fragments.)

How does the United States Government feel about the silencers? "We have checked a number of these cases." Colonel P. Freeman, Pentagon spokesman for Project Blue Book was quoted as saying, "and these men are not connected with the Air Force in any way."

Nor will any other United States security group claim them. It has never been within the line of duty of any government agency to threaten a private citizen or to enter his home without permission or a search warrant. No government agent is empowered to demand surrender of private property by any law-abiding citizen.

Colonel Freeman went on to say that by posing as Air Force officers and government agents, the silencers are committing a federal offence.

"We would like to catch one," he told John Keel. "Unfortunately, the trail is always too cold by the time we hear about these cases. But we are still trying."

Pursuit by government agencies has done little to slow down the activities of the silencers. In 1967, four bogus Air Force officers assembled policemen and civilians who had witnessed heavy UFO activity in Wanaque, New Jersey and told them that they "hadn't seen a thing." Sternly, the citizens of Wanaque were admonished not to discuss the sightings over the Wanaque Reservoir with anyone.

Californian Rex Heflin managed to take some highly interesting photos of a UFO while performing his duties with the highway department. A few days later Heflin was visited by a man bearing credentials of the North American Air Defence. The phony NORAD investigator demanded and received, Heflins original series of pictures.

In April, 1966, two Norwalk, Connecticut, schoolboys were pursued by a low-flying UFO. The next day a man appeared at the boys' school and introduced himself to the principal as a representative of a "government agency so secret that he couldn't give the name". The mysterious agent questioned the boys for nearly three hours.

Broadcaster Frank Edwards, now best known for his best selling FLYING SAUCERS - SERIOUS BUSINESS, made much of the official "plot" that had been set to silence him.

Before he became interested in UFO'S Edward had been conducting a highly successful radio show sponsored by the American Federation of Labour. He was warned to abandon the subject. Edwards persisted and was given his walking papers. In spite of the thousands of letters which protested the firing of Edwards and the silencing of his UFO reports, his ex- sponsors stood firm.

When reporters asked George Meany, President of the AFL, why Edwards had been dropped, Meany answered: "Because he talked too much about flying saucers!" Edwards said that he later learned that his constant mention of UFO'S had been irritating to the Defence Department and that that department had brought pressure to bear on the AFL.

Edwards was only temporarily silenced. He soon had in syndication a radio show that dealt almost exclusively with flying saucers and other phenomena. News of the sudden death of Frank Edwards stunned delegates assembled for the 1967 Congress of Scientific UFOlogists in New York Cities Hotel Commodore on June 24th. The date was a significant one. Twenty years before, Kenneth Arnold had made the UFO sighting near Mt. Rainier, Washington that gave the term "flying saucers" to our language. The thoughts of several flying saucer researchers turned at once to "the silencers."

"Edwards was warned to lay off UFO investigation" one delegate suggested. "He had been visited by the same three MIBs that shut up Albert K. Bender."

"Nonsense!" said another. "Frank has been ill for six months. Besides that, he was overweight and working too hard. It was only natural that the heart of a man in his fifties would begin to feel the pace that Edwards was setting."

"Not true!" argued yet another ufologist. "Frank has never been ill. Check the obituary. It reads death was 'apparently' due to a heart attack. How many other researchers have died of an "apparent" something or other?"

Jack Robinson, assistant editor of SAUCER NEWS, said: "On two occasions an electronic-type voice, definitely not human, has told me to stop all saucer research. It sounded like the strange kind of "voice" that might be produced by a Voder machine. Each time the phone calls have come, the message has been the same: "Stop all saucer research."

Timothy Green Beckley, director of "Searchlight", a UFO news service, told us: "I have never received other than kook calls myself, but I am currently investigating two cases that involve dark- complexioned men who have silenced flying saucer sighters in Oregon and Texas."

Howard Menger, who claims to have been inside a flying saucer and to have talked with the aliens inside, said, "When I was living in High Bridge, New Jersey, in 1957, the men in dark business suits came to call on me. They flashed authentic looking credentials and claimed to be from a government bureau."

"They looked like like ordinary people. One wore glasses. They warned me to quit talking to me about flying saucers and to drop my research. We had quite an argument, and they claimed to have considerable power. Whether this was power of influence or of strange powers beyond those of ordinary people, I don't know. Eventually they left."

Menger went on. "These same MIBs have visited other researchers. They sometimes claim to be Air Force representatives or agents from various other governmental bureaus. They are definitely not affiliated with the Air Force or the government and these imposters have created a situation for which the Air Force is blamed.

"Both the Air Force and the CIA are taking a beating from public opinion on things done by these imposters. "These imposters visit people who have contacted or seen flying saucers. They come into a sighters or a contactee's home and take any films that might of been made of flying saucers. They state that the film will be developed by the government labs. When the imposters leave and the citizen never receives his film back, he blames the Air Force or the CIA!"

There will be many researchers, however, who will not be so quick to absolve the Air Force or government security agencies from all duplicity in the silencings of key UFO witnesses. In the October, 1966, issue of "Flying Saucers", Ray Palmer ran the story "Navy Claps Saucer Sighters in Psychiatric Ward!" This article detailed the plight of seaman Gary Steven Trent and Charles Lester Niblick, Jr., who were "reassigned" to Ward T-11 of the Philadelphia Naval Hospital after spotting UFO'S in the spring of 1966.

Recently, a number a researchers have been plagued by an unpleasant manifestation associated with the silencers that has come to be known familiarity as "the smellies"

Here is a typical case that occurred to a prominent ufologist in October, 1967. The entire family was seated in- front of the television set when their dog began to raise a rumpus, punctuated by "ungodly howls". The animal crawled on its belly, snarling, terribly frightened, yet instinctively compelled to protect the household. The dog jumped up, charged, was forced backward. The family was amazed. There was absolutely no visible thing that their dog could be attacking. Then came the "smelly" - a terrible stench that permeated the entire house in a sustained, nauseating "gas attack" lasting for about one minute. The odor was so powerful, that the family had all they could do to refrain from bolting outside and leaving their home to their unseen and savory invader.

One researcher reported regular attacks by a "smelly" at precisely the same time each day for more than eight consecutive days.

Added to this phenomenon have been reports of contact via television. A number of individuals who have sighted UFO'S have claimed later communication with "aliens" through their home television sets. The aliens frequency disrupts normal programming to allow robed figures to instruct the saucer sighters to co-operate with the aliens and to keep their information confidential. In exchange for the saucer sighters silence and co- operation, the aliens promises him that he will be allowed to work with them on certain glorious secret projects for the betterment of mankind.

Whether such stories are born of individual delusion or organized deception, the authors have received reports of these communication from nearly every section of the US. Here is a typical report of such a contact that was sent to the editorial office of "Saucer Scoop".

"...Now to the Organization; I have been working for them for four years. They first contacted me right after I had two unusual UFO sightings - one in which three large, blue, glowing saucers landed near my house (later I went up to the site and found landing gear depressions) and the next on the following Sunday when I saw a huge silver saucer which hovered 20 feet above me and seemed to be taking my picture! Next you ask how they contacted me... They had and perfected a magnetic frequency equal to the VHF stations on TV. And so one night when they were ready and I was home alone watching TV, they cut in on channel 3 and cut off the normal transmission... by means of a director beam and transmitted to me. Using the magnetic wave principal, they told me how to construct an mg transmitter of my own...

"...Though I have never met any of them personally, I know where their base is in my area and i've watched their activity from a distance by telescope, in addition to seeing them on my TV."

This particular contactee identified the Organization as the "United Planets Council". According to him, "...their saucers have been landing on Earth for thousands of years. They are studying Earth and waiting until Earth can put spaceships on the moon - then Earth will be asked to join the UPC. Science will advance tremendously..."

Those who put credence in such reports are divided into two camps concerning their correct interpretation. There are the cosmic positive thinkers who sincerely believe such contacts to be initiated by the benign "space brothers" in order to better prepare man for the glories of the "new age" of interplanetary brotherhood. Then there are those who feel that such privileged communication from the Organization is but an elaborate ploy to insure the silence of those who have witnessed certain saucer sightings. Those who hold this view also believe that there is at least one UFO group which is, at best, indifferent to the fate of Homo Sapiens and which may even be hostile to Earths inhabitants.

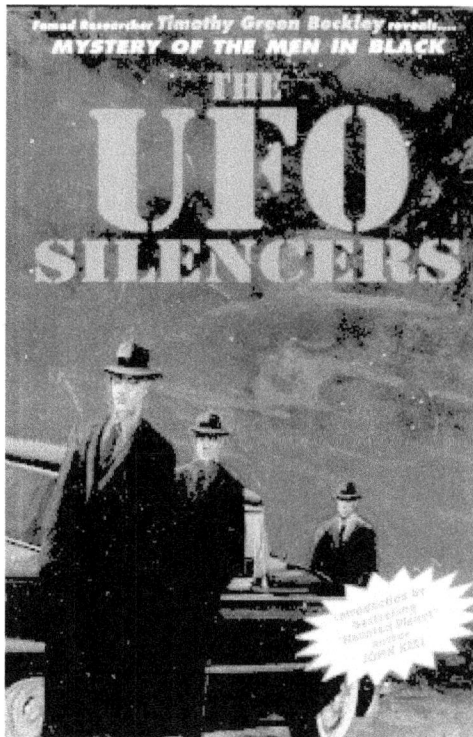

Researcher Robert A. Stiff recently advised: "Check your past copies of "Saucer Scoop" and other UFO publications and see how many cases are reported that suggest outright hostility and attack by the UFO's, based on fact and how many others report friendly contact with our "space brothers". You will find that the former outweighs the latter by a wide margin.

"The aliens have been reported to have even waved at us in a friendly manner from their craft" Stiff continued. "I, too have done the same thing. The only difference was that I waved at animals in a cage! I was being friendly to dumb animals for my own amusement. When you stop to think about it there may be no difference. We, too, may be dumb creatures providing amusement for others while they attain their goal. Our government knows more about the UFO's than they are willing to say, and they must have a serious reason. The only time we are SUPPOSED to be deceived by our government is when National security is at stake. Is this the case concerning UFO's? If so, the answer is at hand. Friends do not cause occurrences which would involve national security."

Stiff has come to feel that the aura of laughter built up around persons claiming contact with aliens has been a deliberate action on the part of those who would have the truth withheld from the public.

"Again the big question, why?" Stiff asks, "What is there about UFO's that must be kept silent - not to be disclosed? What path are we as UFOlogists following that is evidently leading to something important - so important that we must be quieted? Why the harassment of prominent UFO authorities? The privacy of them is no longer sacred and telephones have become the object of distrust.

"Wild imagination? A most definite and sad NO! We have reached the point where the serious study of UFO's has become a battle!"

Are the silencers horror or hoax? And if it is all a hoax, who is perpetrating it all, and more importantly, why? Just exactly what is the silence group that is determined to make a sinister battleground of flying saucer research?

Are they, in spite of official denials, agents from a top-secret US government agency, which knows the answer to the UFO enigma and has been commissioned to keep the truth from the public?

Could they be agents from another terrestrial political system that endeavors to guard its secret for just a bit longer?

Or, as some Researchers have theorized, could the silencers and the UFO'S be coming from an older terrestrial race which has survived and become more technically advanced as it thrives in some remote place on Earth?

Why do the silencers want certain UFO investigations discontinued? Why do they so desperately want the nations of the world to remain ignorant of the true facts about flying saucers?

It may be because they realise the more ignorant man is of the true dangers which face him, the less able he is to deal with the crisis situation. The less prepared man is to handle the inevitable confrontation with an alien race, the more rapidly he will allow himself, slave-like, to become subject to a race or culture which considers itself to be superior to Homo Sapiens.

Eminent psychologist C.G. Jung wrote with great insight when, he said: "We would be placed in the very questionable position of today's primitive societies that clash with the superior cultures of the white race. All initiative would be wrested from us. As an old witch doctor once said to me, with tears in his eyes, "We will have no more dreams."

"Our science and technology would go on the junk pile. What such a catastrophe would mean morally we can gauge only by the pitiful decline of primitive cultures that has taken place before our very eyes."

How much longer will the mysterious silencers continue in their attempts to squelch saucer research? How long before the MIB's are exposed or willingly cast off their black suits in favor of material uniform? And if the mysterious silence group should in time prove themselves to be citizens of an alien culture, how much longer will they continue to knock on doors, give ominous and unsolicited advice over telephones and harass UFO researchers before they begin invading our world?

Courtesy of UFOEvidence.com

The MIB come in all shapes and sizes as is illustrated by artist
Carol Ann Rodriguez who envisions one of The Silencers.

# HORRIFIC UNSEEN FORCES

Source: www.alien-ufos.com

## Here is proof the Men in Black come in all shapes and sizes and may come after YOU! next.

**Dogtown, near Evansville Indiana**
**Date: August 21 1955**
**Time: afternoon**

Mrs. Darwin Johnson was swimming with her friend Mrs. Chris Lamble in the Ohio River about fifteen feet from shore when suddenly something grabbed her from under the surface. It felt like the "hand" had huge claws and "furry" palms. It came up from behind her, grabbed her left leg, gripped her knee and pulled her under. She kicked and fought herself free. It pulled her under again. Although both women could not see the thing, they were screaming and yelling to scare it away. Finally, Mrs. Johnson lunged for Mrs. Lamble's inner tube, and the loud "thump" apparently scared it away, as if released its grip. Back on shore Mrs. Johnson received treatment for her scratches and marks on her legs. According to Fortean investigator Terry Colvin Mrs. Johnson had a palm-print shaped green stain below her knee that could not be removed for several days. **Interestingly Colvin learned that an individual who identified himself as an Air Force colonel visited the Johnson couple. He took voluminous notes and warned them not to talk further about the incident.**

**Fort Erie, Ontario, Canada**
**Date: 1956**
**Time: various**

Years after the incident the witness recalled that as a young boy he was visited in his bedroom on several occasions by several men dressed in black that would take him out of the room while his parents slept. They would perform tests on him and it was almost always on his spinal cord. On several occasions he attempted to scream but was unable to. **The dark garbed "doctors" warned him that he should never speak of them or else he would be in danger.** The "treatments" continued for a while then finally just stopped. The witness has peculiar "scars" on his back to this day.

**Near Gorman California**
**Date: June 1956**
**Time: night**

Jan Whitley was driving along a mountain road with Emily Cronin and the latter's six-year-old son who was sleeping in the back seat. They pulled off at a rest stop to sleep awhile. They remembered seeing a light resembling a truck headlight at first; also they heard a high-pitched whining sound and felt paralyzed. Both felt the car sway for an unknown reason. Emily perceived a mental message telling her that someone was going to take her away.

Then she saw a man looking in the back window of the car. Under hypnosis Emily recalled seeing a tall humanoid with a thin face and wearing black clothes, which was looking into the car apparently fascinated by the sight of the little boy. Two other beings tried to call away their curious companion. Emily understood the conversation among them to say that the encounter was a mistake, but the curious being shook the car and continued his observations, despite the other's objections. The witnesses eventually managed to leave the site, but later were unable to locate the exact spot alongside the road.

## Biggelswade England
## Date: November 28 1956
## Time: night

A strange customer in his shop, with a very high forehead, told John Whitworth that he could see a flying saucer if he would go to a certain spot on November 28. Whitworth went and did see hovering an object like a humming top, with lighted portholes. Just one year later the visitor returned & told him he would have a contact this time, at another spot. Whitworth went with a crowd of others, including a BBC recording van, & was disappointed. **Later a telephone call, "in an unearthly voice" reproached him from bringing the others**

## Aberdeen, Washington
## Date: Summer 1959
## Time: afternoon

On a Friday afternoon Shirley Teabo was driving to her home in the suburbs of Seattle when she barely noticed a tall, angular man hunched at the shoulder of a curving stretch of highway, she had never before picked up a hitchhiker yet for some reason she felt an inner compulsion to offer this man a lift. Almost without volition she backed her car along the shoulder of the freeway, but began to tremble with fright when he slid into the seat beside her. "Don't be afraid, Shirley," she reports that he said. She wondered how he knew her name.

She noted other odd things about her new companion. Although it was a steaming summer day, he wore a heavy pinstriped suit with wide out of date lapels, and a wide brimmed black hat pulled low over his eyes. Suddenly he was telling her things about herself that she had never told anyone, and she had the weird sensation that she had known him all her life. Increasingly suspicious, she pulled into a roadside restaurant area, hoping that the hitchhiker would look for another ride. But he followed her inside, and sat quietly while she ordered coffee and an ice-cream cone, declining anything for himself.

She offered the stranger ice cream and he appeared to study the cone for a long time before tasting it. They returned to the car, and were cruising through Tacoma before Shirley realized that she had no idea of her passenger's destination. "Oh, this will be fine," he said vaguely. She stopped the car, and he smiled and called good-bye. As she pulled back onto the roadway she glanced in the rearview mirror for a last glimpse of the stranger. But he was gone. She pulled off the road, looking frantically up and down the highway. There was nowhere for him to hide, yet he was nowhere to be seen. He had vanished. Another man, a neighbor known as Everett reported a very similar encounter with an equally described and garbed man who also mysteriously disappeared after a short car ride.

## Pennsylvania, exact location not given
## Date: Summer 1959
## Time: late evening

The witness was sitting in his lounge chair, reading, dozing but was at the same time tense and restless. Something seemed to be at the back of his mind. Suddenly he looked toward the door. Somehow he knew someone was at the other side. He lay his book down got up and went to the door, opened it a crack and looked out.

There were two men dressed in black there. They looked like identical twins. They were dark complexioned with Oriental eyes, but they were definitely not Orientals. They never said a word but the witness heard in his mind, "Are you ready?" He does not know why but for some reason he was ready to go. Since it was so terribly hot that night, he had stripped down to his "birthday suit" so when he reached for a pair of walking shorts again he heard in his mind, "That will not be necessary. No one will see you."

They stepped out in the hall and instantly they were on top of a flat hill in back of the apartments. The witness was rather surprised that the scene had changed so quickly. He noticed the headlights of a car coming down the street, and he ducked behind the two men. He then heard some laughter in his mind, "We told you no one would see you. Try it." He then boldly stepped around in front of them, spread his feet apart, propped his hands on his hips, daring anyone to see me.

But the car, with a man and a woman in it, passed a few feet from them not even looking in their direction. He turned to say something to his companions and they were looking up. He followed their gaze and realized that something was hanging there suspended above them. As he did so, an opening appeared in its center and blue-white light came tumbling out of it. He felt a queasy sensation in the pit of his stomach, like when you are in an elevator or an airplane that is dropping too fast. He could see apartment houses and the ground receding below them. They were floating up toward whatever the object was. He blacked out as they approached the opening.

When he came to he was lying on his side facing a wall. He rolled over on his back and sat up. He was in an oddly shaped room. It somehow resembled a wedge of pie with the point of bitten off. The whole room was bare except for some kind of projection on which he was sitting. Everything seemed to be made out of a blue gray material. While the walls were very hard the surface on he was sitting was very soft even though everything seemed to have been made of the same material. The room was bathed in a soft glow and there were no shadows anywhere, but there was no light source that he could see. He then heard a female voice say, "He's awake now."

He looked around to see if he could spot the speaker but saw nothing, just the walls. About this time on the short wall a door appeared and opened. He could see into a hallway. Although the hall was dark, here was blue-white illumination that appeared as though it was coming from some great distance. Two shadows flittered across the doorway. He couldn't tell anything about their shapes.

The movement was too rapid and too distorted. But he received a mental impression of two people approaching---a man in the front and a woman in the back---carrying a tray full of some kind of surgical instruments and hypodermic syringes. His next memory was of being back in his apartment, in his chair, reading his book. An interesting detail was that a book that he had been reading went mysteriously missing for a week after the encounter and was later found right on the same spot where the witness had left it.

### Brands Flat Virginia
### Date: January 19 1965
### Time: 1815

William Blackburn was chopping firewood in preparation for an archery match when he noticed a large conical object in the sky, which he judged to be 240 feet in diameter. While he watched it, he saw a similar but smaller UFO, 60 ft wide, with a bubble-like cupola on top, land 50 ft away. It was made out of metal polished to a mirror finish. A pie like section opened out and three small entities only 3 ft tall emerged and floated toward him. They were dressed in close fitting uniforms of the same high polish as the UFO, and wore shoes with 3 or 4-inch soles. Their skin was of an orange red color, and one had "a long finger on his left hand." Their faces were human like in appearance. These beings approached to within 12 ft and addressed him in a language that the witness could not understand. When he made no reply, the little men re-entered their vehicle, and both objects then rapidly disappeared. The sighting occurred during a localized wave of reports in the area, and **the witness was subsequently asked by an un-named government agency not to discuss his sighting further.**

### Caliham, Texas
### Date: June 6 1965
### Time: 0245A

The 5-year old witness woke up in the middle of the night on his way to cuddle into bed with his parents as he usually did late at night. However, that night he saw bright lights in the house and hid in the crawl space between the refrigerator and the wall.

He then saw 2 dull bright figures that were maybe 3 ft tall with glowing eyes. This frightened him and he covered his face with his hands. However he still peeked through his fingers and realized that he was now face to face with the figures. He then ran to his sister's room and hid under the covers in between his two sisters. **The witness claims that the next day his home was visited by "men in black suits" who asked all kinds of questions pertaining to lights and fires near the barn area.**

**Birmingham, England**
**Date: December 1965**
**Time: night**

One night Margery was told by her first husband to prepare for a shock and some kind of test. It was obvious that he was being quite serious. They got into his car and drove off, although her memory of the trip became hazy and confused and she does not know where they went. Then she was in a room that was dimly lit and there were people standing around a long table or flat bed. She was put onto it and seemed "drugged" and unable to resist. The most memorable of the men in the group was tall and thin with a long nose and white beard. He had thick eyebrows and supposedly said to Margery. "Remember the eyebrows, honey." A strange medical examination, using odd equipment, was performed on her. Her husband then took her on a trip to all the houses she would occupy in the future. This was accomplished by a click of the fingers, followed by a barrage of images. Her mind was filled with information but she was told that she would remember it only bit by bit as the future unfolded. The memory of the experience did return only from 1978 onwards. At one point one of the "examiners" in the room said to Margery, in a tone that made it seem as he were amused, "They will think its flying saucers." Her husband also revealed who he really was---but she declined to tell the investigator or source. The day after the "abduction" to a house somewhere in Birmingham her husband left, said he was going abroad, and Margery never saw or heard from him again.

Here are reports of MIBs, MIB like individuals and others that seem intent on retriving artifact(s), photo(s), in intimidating or silencing the witness(s) in some way. Some seem only to be watchers...

I encourage others to look for earlier reports and post them if you can...

**Los Angeles California**
**Date: February 1953**
**Time: afternoon**

A pair of strange looking men, described as over 6' 2" tall, visited a local attorney's office. Wearing old tattered clothing, with bluish-green skin tone and peculiar looking pointy ears. Both men claimed they were experts at locating "missing persons." At one point one of the men made a deep wedge with his bare hands into the top of a metallic cabinet of at least half an inch in depth. Unnerved by their strange behavior employees called the local FBI office, but upon the arrival of the agents, the two enigmatic strangers had totally vanished.

## Kentucky, exact location not given
## Date: Summer 1954
## Time: afternoon

A couple eating supper at a local restaurant saw a strange "man" or entity sitting in the back of the restaurant. The man was sitting still with his hands on his knees, he was very tall, & his head and shoulders were higher than any other person there. He was silent & sat still staring at everyone. He wore a dark brown suit; he apparently noticed the witnesses looking at him, gout up and walked out. He wore very peculiar five toed dark brown shoes and had a very narrow heel.

## Quarouble France
## Date: September 10 1954
## Time: 2230

Hearing his dogs barking, Marius Dewilde went out and saw a dark mass on the railroad track, less than 6 yards away. On hearing footsteps, he turned his flashlight on the path, where he saw 2 very short beings (less than 3.5 ft) wearing "diver's suits." No arms could be seen. He approached within 6 ft, when he was blinded and paralyzed by a brilliant light emanating from the mass of the tracks. The two creatures went toward the object. When the beam of paralyzing light went out, he ran towards the track, but the object was now rising, emitting a "thick dark steam" and a low whistling sound. It became red luminous and flew away. On the railroad ties where found 5 imprints; it was calculated that a 30-ton weight would have been necessary to produce them. Recent information uncovered about the case indicates that Dewilde found after the craft took off a mysterious metallic black box. He took the box home and attempted to open it, without telling local police about it. After several failed attempts he finally gave up and hid the black box inside a carton. **According to Dewilde shortly after this several French Air Force officers who somehow knew about the existence of the black box and took possession of it visited him.** (I doubt they were who they said they were)

## Raon-l 'Etape, Vosges France
## Date: October 20 1954
## Time: 0230A

Lazlo Ujvari, going to work late at night, encountered a heavy set man of medium height wearing a gray jacket with insignias on the shoulders, and a motorcycle helmet, which threatened him with a revolver and spoke words he did not understand. Ujvari spoke Russian to him and got a reply in that language. The unknown man then asked whether he was in Spain or Italy; then, what time it was. '0230", said Ujvari. "You lie," replied the man, taking out his own watch and announcing "Four o'clock!" He then escorted Ujvari past an inverted dish shaped, lightless saucer bearing a 2-foot antenna, which took up almost the whole width of the road. After 30 yards, he said, he said 'Adieu!" After a few paces, Ujvari looked back; with a whine like an electric motor, the saucer rose vertically.

## Hamilton New Zealand
## Date: December 1954
## Time: 0130A

Doreen Wilkinson reported that three invisible entities attacked and violated her in her home. Around the same time John Stuart was sitting at his desk when a bizarre entity appeared before him. The humanoid was about four or five ft from him and was facing him. Its body resembled, vaguely that of a human. From the waist up it was a man and from the waist down that of a woman. Its flesh stinking putrid, seemed to hang in folds. It was grayish color. The slack mouth was dribbling, its lips moved but there was no sound. Stuart heard a telepathic message, "Your friend knew too much and had to be silenced." Soon the creature seemed to waver and grow less distinct; then materialized again into solidity. Stuart almost collapsed in horror as he realized that the male & female areas of its body had changed places. He received one more warning before the creature dissolved and disappeared. Stuart soon abandoned Ufology.

## Wildwood New Jersey
## Date: January 9 1967
## Time: 1730

At 1730 there was a knock at the Edward Christiansen residence (involved in a previous UFO encounter), 17-year old Connie Christiansen when to the door, stunned she reported back, "It's the strangest looking man I've ever seen." Mrs Christiansen went to the door, unbolted, and unlatched it. It was growing dark and was bitter cold outside. There was no car in view and this seemed peculiar because the Christiansen home was removed from other houses in a rather isolated spot. A tall man stood at the door, he asked if Edward Christiansen lived there. And then said he was from "the Missing Heirs Bureau" and asked to be led in. The stranger was then invited him.

The visitor must have been at least 6'6" tall, enormously broad. He wore a Russian fur hat with a black visor on it and a very long black coat that seemed to be made out of thin material, too thin for the cold weather. He told the family "this will only take forty minutes." As he removed his hat he revealed an unusual head, large and round while his face seemed angular, pointed. He had black hair, which was closely cropped, to his head. There was a perfectly round spot on the back of his head as if that area had recently been shaved. His nose and mouth seemed relatively normal, but his eyes were large, protruding, like "thyroid eyes," and set wide apart. One eye appeared to have a cast, like a glass eye, and did not move in unison with is companion.

During the course of the conversation Mr. Christiansen noticed a badge on the stranger's shirt pocket, which he quickly covered with his hand and removed, placing it in his coat pocket. It resembled a gold or brass badge and it seemed to have a big K on it with a small x alongside and letters and numbers around the edge, according to Connie Christiansen. Underneath his thin outer coat he was wearing a short-sleeved shirt made of a Dacron like material. His trousers were of a dark material gray or black, and were a little too short. He wore dark shoes with unusually thick rubber soles.

A strange feature on his leg fascinated Mrs Christiansen & Connie. When he sat down they could see a long thick green wire attached to the inside of his leg. It came up out or his socks and disappeared under his trousers. At one point it seemed to be indented into his leg and was covered with a large brown spot. The Christiansen's noted that the visitor had an unnatural pallor. His speech was also strange, with a high "tinny" voice that seemed especially peculiar coming from such a large man. He also spoke in a strange, hard to understand, singsong like manner. At one point as his face gradually grew redder he asked for a glass of water and swallowed a large yellow capsule which he gulped down. He then returned to normal.

After about 40 minutes he donned his hat and coat and told Mr. Christiansen that he would be in touch. When he reached the road, he made a gesture and a black 1963 Cadillac drove through the trees and pulled up. He climbed into the car and it drove away with its headlights off.

## Pittsfield, Pennsylvania
## Date: January 25 1967
## Time: around 1800

On January 20 at 2330 Mrs. Walter J Kushner and her two daughters, Susan (17) and Tanya (14) and a close friend of the girls, Marianne Williamson (16), witnessed a brilliant aero form with a distinct disk shape drop below the cloud cover and execute a sharp turn before cruising parallel to a mountain ridge while the group was returning to their residence.

All members of the party were awed by the lack of the sound and high speed of the object. On January 21 1967 @ 0200A, Susan, Tanya and Marianne were enjoying a typical teenage pajama party and were doing anything but sleeping when all three girls simultaneously spotted a peculiar light shimmering through the closed curtains of Susan's bedroom. Without warning the drapes parted of their own volition and a midget triangular object hovering a few feet from the house began beaming pinkish light of a painfully brilliant intensity into the bedroom. When the triangle moved to the second window, the curtains repeated their opening act and the intensity of light emanating from the object increased several fold. At this point the girls became quite frightened and decided to get the hell out of there.

Suddenly, all three girls became paralyzed and weak, unable to cry out or do more than whimper helplessly. Not able to move, their terror at this point became so strong that prayer became a viable option. After a few more torturous moments that seemed like an eternity, the light effect dissipated and their freedom of movement was restored, although a weird dizzy sensation continued to haunt the girls for the better part of an hour.

On the 28th things were back to normal when shortly after the dinner hour, two men arrived at the Kushner household. They identified themselves as military investigators and flashed what appeared to be USAF identification. Mrs. Kushner described the ID card as having black printing on a durable white stock. Both men wore tan trench coats, which they kept buttoned from knee to collar. The taller of the two, who, according to the family's testimony, did all the talking, was described, as having blond hair, green eyes, was thin and deeply tanned. The other gentleman was heavyset with dark hair, piercing blue eyes and was also deeply tanned.

The men were very polite but very insistent about one thing: they wanted every shred of information about the girl's experience. Neither parent could explain why they allowed their children to be so intensely grilled by these "government agents." The men moved about the house with apparently total knowledge of the whereabouts of rooms, furniture, objects, etc. Their clothing looked as if it had been purchased 10 minutes before and the bottom of their shoes seemed un-walked on. When the mystery men left, they backed their vehicle out onto the roadway turned off their headlights and powered away down the road. At one point one of the men was seen writing strange symbols in vertical columns, starting from the left, going down one column, up the next, down the third. This on a small booklet. (Typical MIB report of the period).

## Owatonna, Minnesota
## Date: May 1967
## Time: evening

One man, five-foot-nine inches tall, with olive complexion and pointed face and long dark hair (too long for Air Force regulations or so the Butlers felt) arrived at the Butler household and identified himself as Air Force Major Richard French. Speaking perfect English and plainly well educated, he claimed that he was interested in CB (citizen's band) radio and UFOs.

He was dressed in a neat gray suit, white shirt and black tie and everything he owned appeared to be brand new. Even the soles of his shoes were un-scuffed and un-walked on. He drove a white Ford Mustang. "He said his stomach was bothering him," said Mrs. Butler, who then told the air force officer that what he needed was some Jell-o. He said if it kept bothering him, he would come back for some. Major French returned to the Butler residence the next morning. His stomach was still bothering him, so Mrs. Butler slid a big bowl of Jell-o in front of him. Incredibly, according to Mrs. Butler, Major

French picked up the bowl and attempted to drink it. She had to show him how to eat it with a spoon.

## Mount Misery Long Island New York
## Date: May 18 1967
## Time: 1030A

The day after being instructed by a metallic sounding voice in her phone to go to the small local public library, Jane Paro did as was instructed. The library was deserted except for the librarian, who stuck Jane as being unusual. The woman was "dressed in an old fashioned suit like something out of the 1940's with a long skirt, broad shoulders, and flat old looking shoes." She had a dark complexion, with a fine bone structure, and very black eyes and hair. When Jane entered, the woman seemed to be expecting her and produced a book instantly form under the desk. Jane sat down at a table and began to riffle through the book, pausing on page 42.

The metallic voice had told her to read that page. Suddenly the print became smaller and smaller, then larger and larger. It changed into a message about contact with earthlings. The print became very small again, and then the normal text reappeared. As soon as Jane left the library she became quite ill. In early June she began to see the "librarian" wherever she went. Unable to sleep one night, Jane gout up at the crack of dawn the following morning and went for a walk on an impulse. The dark skinned woman stepped out of an alley and approached her shyly. "Peter is coming," she                                                                      announced.
Jane asked her a question and she repeated, "Peter is coming very soon." Next a large black Cadillac came down the street and stopped next to them. It was brand new, very shiny, and polished. The driver was an olive skinned man wearing wraparound sunglasses and dressed in a neat gray suit, apparently of the same material as the woman's clothes. The rear door opened and a man climbed out with a big grin on his face. He was about five-feet 8 inches tall, with dark skin and Oriental eyes. He had an air of someone very important and was dressed in a well-cut, expensive looking suit of the same gray material that was shiny like silk but was not silk. The stranger said his name was "Apol."

## Chimney Rock Colorado
## Date: mid June 1967
## Time: afternoon

A month after seeing a strange crescent shaped light over the Great Sand Dunes National Monument and painting a picture of the light, the witness; Mrs Blundell was visited by a strange character at the Pine Cove Inn. The man was deathly pale, had very dark hair, and wore a dark suit. He told Mrs Blundell that he was not from our universe and could not read but could name the contents of any book in any library. He expressed interest in obtaining the picture of the light, but said he had no money and would return on a later date. The strange visitor then departed in a vehicle with Arizona license plates. He was not seen again.

## Cordoba Argentina
## Date: June 21 1967
## Time: daytime?

Four days prior of a massive wave of UFO sightings in the region a man dressed in black showed up at the newsroom of Cordoba's, "Los Principios" daily, where he dropped off a letter addressed to the editor stating that before the week was out the Southern Cone would experience a massive fly over involving hundreds of extraterrestrial craft. The day before the sighting began, the newspaper received a phone call stating, "Attention, it will begin at any moment..."

## Greenland, Long Island, New York
## Date: October 1967
## Time: early morning

Awakened by the sounds of his dogs barking Joseph Henslik looked outside and was surprised to see a strange circular object circling over the post office building near his house. Reacting quickly he grabbed his camera and ran to the patio. He took several photos of the luminous disc-shaped object that appeared to have a turret on top on which he could see several lighted windows. Two days after once he had obtained the negatives two strange men visited Henslik at his home. After returning home at about 0300A that morning he noticed that two men were waiting for him. He described them as being of medium height, black hair and very tanned skin. Both wore very tight-fitting black slacks; black turtle necked sweaters and what appeared to be a black "smoking" jacket. One of the men approached Henslik and in a strange Scandinavian sounding accent he told him that they were representatives of the government and that they needed to speak to him

They refused to show him any credentials since they claimed to belong to a "top secret government agency". The stranger told him, "We know that you took some photographs that can be considered authentic and in the name of your family, the government and the world (!) We request you give those to us". Henslik told them that he did not have the photos yet, the men then left promising to return the next day. Precisely at the same time the next day Henslik received another visit, this time from three similarly dressed strangers, totally dressed in black. Afraid Henslik gave them the negatives, which they examined closely with a flashlight, then, warned him not to tell anyone about the photos and walked away into the darkness. Henslik was surprised since he did not see a vehicle or any other mode of transportation in the area.

# EXPLORING THE MIB FLAP IN UK BY ANDREW LUNN

### British UFO Research Assoc. and ISUR

This section explores the myth of the MIB (Men In Black). It is mainly based on my MIB research regarding incidents after 1976 in England.

## Part 1:
## The Making of the Myth

Many seem to feel it was divisions of the USAF that created the MIB myth, but this could not be further from the truth. There is strong evidence to suggest that MIB have been co-existing with us, since we care to remember and this leads one to ask why there was ever such a need. The actual basis of their origin lies deep within the recesses of the UFO witness, as research suggests that MIB normally make an appearance after somebody has witnessed a UFO. This has often led me to believe whether the ability to see a UFO, brings out the MIB from their hiding, forced to contemplate the inevitable that their hidden origin will be revealed one day. However this is even harder to believe when faced with the MIB themselves; a shocking confrontation whereby the witness is unsure of how to act, due to the weirdness being exhibited by the strange guests. The actual name Men in black is misleading, as there have been sightings reported to me of Females in black; this may lead one to think that maybe they do possess some Alien origin, capable of taking on any form they like.

I tend to back away from the alien hypothesis mainly due to my consistent analysis of English cases pre 1976, which tend to emphasis a more direct link with military, normally RAF or MoD. Looking at American reports seem to emphasise a more alien account, and it is here when the issue becomes confusing. It would surely be a lot easier for the government to make use of the MIB, instead of spending copious amounts of time and money necessary for carrying out such widespread operations against people seeing lights in the sky. However there is clear evidence, which will be discussed later on, in which witnesses to UFO's or even top secret government projects have been severely harassed. Much has been born out of this myth, and I feel that around the 1960's, the US government was able to use some of the personnel from the Air Force Special Activities Centre(AFSAC), and 'disguise' them as MIB. Even Mothman(see The Mothman Prophecies by John A. Keel) was part of the MIB myth, and thus their identity becomes ever more tightly kept due to the natural progression that we do nothing to halt proceedings; MIB are natural to human folklore.

# Part 2:
# Common Characteristics of the Modern Day MIB

While most MIB reports tend to highlight the fact that MIB may be of some oriental origin, the detraction is made through the association that MIB always come in threes. Is this irrelevant? Why? Maybe due to the fact that transmogrification takes place, and size/quantity/appearance is irrelevant, in that what you see is what you get, but not necessarily what you want! The classic conception of an MIB is a man of indefinite age, medium height and dressed completely in black. He always has a black hat and often a black turtleneck sweater. They present an appearance often described as "strange" or "odd". They speak in a dull monotone voice, "like a computer", and are dark; complete with high cheekbones, thin lips, pointed chin, and eyes that tend to look oriental like. Often when quizzed as to who they are, they say they are salesman, telephone repairman(even though your phone is not broken) or representatives from official(ie RAF) groups or an unofficial UFO group. Their mode of transport differs whether you are in America or England. In America they are often seen driving Buicks or Lincolns(black); it seems to be only the films that portray the MIB using black cadillacs. In England, the cars are normally Jaguars. It is also important to state that not all reports of MIB are that describing a meeting with men of oriental features; some have included men with very Aryan features, with distinguishing blond hair.

A classic MIB case could be highlighted by the 1978 West Kirby case in Liverpool, England. Here the witness JW has described the classic features of the MIB, and seems to suggest some ulterior motive as to why they came in the first place. It seems usual; JW had seen a UFO, and was shortly visited by two men in black (more men were seen sitting in the car), one of which confronted JW, a teenager at the time. "You'd better run on home" said one of the men. The other man who was with our witness said "It's alright he is with me", and they both then walked away from the men in vehicles. Our witness described the man who got out of the car as dressed in dark blue or black, and stranger still, he appeared to be wearing makeup in the form of lip foundation. This has occurred before(lipstick on MIB), but mainly in American reports(e.g. 1976 Maine). If this was not strange enough JW has no memory of the man's lips moving as he was talking. The descriptions that he gives is remarkably similar to other accounts since the 1950's of the men in black. The MIB's are renowned for visiting UFO witnesses and are often keen in trying to encourage the witness to say nothing of their account. Also many MIB reports state that the men were wearing large hats(often too big for them), however the 1978 West Kirby MIB, had no such headgear.

A case that has come of light fairly recently, is that of William Shearer, whose case is being thoroughly investigated by Ufology and Supernatural Studies(01206 286543-Paul Joslin), led by Barbara Fennell and Paul Southcott. On Monday 19th January 1997(4 days after his UFO incident in Essex) Shearer had returned from work and gone to bed as usual. His wife and daughter had popped out, so he had the house to himself. Unable to settle, he came downstairs for a drink, and thought he heard a faint knock at the door. Sure enough, as Shearer approached the door he could see the outline of a tall man through the glass. Shearer opened the door and was faced with a strange sight. The man was around 6'4", and dressed in a dark grey suit and full length coat. He wore a brilliant white shirt(many other reports have suggested that MIB wear a 'new' type of fabric) and a red tie, and was holding a brimmed hat. Another similarly dressed man was standing behind Shearers' wife's car, and appeared to be looking up and down the road, as if to see if anyone was coming. The first man said "Can I speak to you please?" His voice was very deep, and seemed to Shearer to be coming from his chest rather than his mouth. At this stage, the man's gaze was lowered to the floor so Shearer could not see his face. Shearer assumed the men were Jehovah's Witnesses and replied "No, I'm not dressed". The man persisted, and asked again to speak to Shearer, who again declined and asked him to come back later. When the man lifted his head and looked straight at Shearer his first impression was that the man was very ill, as he looked deathly pale. In contrast, the stranger's lips seemed to be tinged red, as if he were wearing lipstick (how can they get it so wrong for so long??). Again the man spoke, this time asking to come in. Shearer stood his ground. After to looking at the second man, the first finally relented and said okay, they would be back later. On reflection, Shearer states that it was "almost as if the two men were talking to each other, but I couldn't hear them" as the second man kept looking at the first and either nodding or gesturing in some way. The men walked towards their car - which was black and according to Shearer "like something straight out of a gangster movie, yet it looked brand new".

Throughout many of the MIB reports I have studied many MIB car number plates are never traceable, and many never existed in the first place - what are the chances of making up a number plate and it being the only one in existence? Shearer also noticed that the men walked awkwardly, as if they were suffering from arthiritis. Shearer was only convinced that these men were the infamous MIB when told by Paul Southcott of USS, until which time he was adamant that they were religious types. On 12th February, Shearer received another visit, this time while he was at work. He got to meet with the MIB at 1:15 am when he heard a knock on the door. The MIB were slightly smaller than the one he had spoken to before, and Shearer immediately knew it was the one standing by his wife's car on their previous visit. Again he was dressed in the dark suit and coat and wore a hat. This time the MIB asked to speak to Shearer by name, and specified that they wanted to talk to him about his UFO sighting, giving exact date and times. Shearer was baffled as to where he had got this information, but refused to let him in. Shearer asked for the mans name and ID, but the MIB ignored him and repeatedly asked to come in. Shearer states that it was almost as if the MIB could only utter a selection of set phrases, since he kept repeating the same questions over and over again, ignoring Shearer's own questions. On this occasion, Shearer was able to get a closer look at the MIB's face, and realised he had no facial hair at all - no eyebrows, eyelashes, or signs of stubble. The visit lasted for about two minutes, and then the office phone rang. Shearer turned to pick up the phone to hold, and turned back, the MIB was gone

Since the night of Shearer's sighting, all the video equipment in his office building has been malfunctioning for no apparent reason. Since the MIB visits,

Shearer has had problems with his phone lines(very very common in reports both in America and England). Clicking sounds can be heard on calls he receives after 4pm, and on many occasions he will pick up the phone only to find out there is no-one at the other end. British Telecom are at a loss, so they say. On the 26th March 1997, Shearer's phone, was completely out of order. No other lines in the area were affected. At the time of writing, he is still waiting for an explanation from BT.

# Part 3:
# MIB & Black Helicopters

Occasion permits oneself to see some sort of connection between the Men In Black and these mysterious black helicopters that seem to be plaguing our skies, but it is far more complex than the colour match! If we are to presume an existence that is 'alien' to us but having a connection with earth far greater than we could imagine, we start to understand a little of the origin of what I like to refer to as the "original MIB". The same sort of theories are being attached to reasons behind the appearance of unmarked dull grey/green/black helicopters, mysteriously hovering over people's back gardens. A number of reports state that witnesses who have caught a glimpse of the pilots of these strange craft are that of oriental origin, and thus a familiar pattern starts to build up. But this shows now direct correlation, until we look at the behaviour and timing of the black helicopter sightings.

We know that MIB are notorious for making an appearance after someone believes they have seen a UFO, and it is from this we can understand a little behind this timing of events and the occurrence of the black helicopters - the majority of mysterious helicopter sightings suggest that the primary witness has seen a UFO, but what must be determined is how 'knowledge' of these facts are 'leaked' out. The co-existence theory explains a little as to how the MIB can be so knowledgeable about a primary witness(for example, MIB have been known to recall memories that only the witness would have known), but this is where a sharp dividing line is drawn when looking for similarities between the MIB and black helicopter sightings. What has been seen is some form of remote viewing being associated with the helicopters gaining 'special' information; more precisely this can be broken down when hearing witnesses explaining seeing one of these helicopters while at the same time having files downloaded from her computer. Is there a connection, and if so how can this be determined? What is more pleasing to the researcher is the fact that we see some need being built up between the two 'organisations' if you like, to gain this special information and it is this that ties the two phenomena together. It is receipt of this knowledge that enables the MIB to gain such a superior advantage over their human counterparts. Without the ability to 'co-exist' and being able to listen but be seen only when it suits them, the MIB would not be associated with UFO phenomena to such a large extent. It is in essence the very basis of their unknown quantity that allows them to stay as outsiders, but involved in everything we do. One must stop short of trying to empathise with something that will never be fully understood and perhaps try to concentrate on the knowledge we do have about the MIB.

Sources:
The Mothman Prophecies - John A. Keel
The Eighth Tower - John A. Keel
Daimonic Reality - Patrick Harpur
Operation Trojan Horse - John A. Keel
Ufology & Supernatural Studies - Barbara Fennell and Paul Southcott
Men In Black Case File - Jim Keith

Film maker Bob Wilkenson shown with material from his Gray Barker collection, part of a film he has made on his favorite UFOlogist whose description of the Men in Black set the stage for generations to come.

# THE MIB AND THE WORLD OF ANNE HENSON BY NICK REDFERN

Here is an MIB report of a slightly different sort as submitted by our friend and associate Nick Redfern who knows as much about the Men in Black as any American researcher.

On the evening of August 30, 1962, the world was about to change drastically for a teenager named Anne Henson when she was plunged into a late-night UFO/bedroom encounter complete with distinct MIB overtones.

When I tracked her down, Henson told me about the incident:

"At the time that this happened, I lived on a dairy farm and was still at school; I was sixteen at the time. I actually moved back here with my family some years ago and we run a nursery business now. It was the middle of the night and something must have woken me up because I sat up in my bed and I could see through the window what looked like a round ball of light in the sky; my room over-looked the Brendon Hills. It seemed to change color from red to green to yellow and I could see a circle with rays of light coming from it.

"At first I thought it was a star, but it wasn't static. Then I thought that it must be a helicopter or something like that, but there was absolutely no sound from it. Well, it then began moving backwards and forwards and went from left to right. I was very intrigued by it because it was making fairly rapid movements. But it was the colors of the lights that attracted me first; they were nice bright colors. It

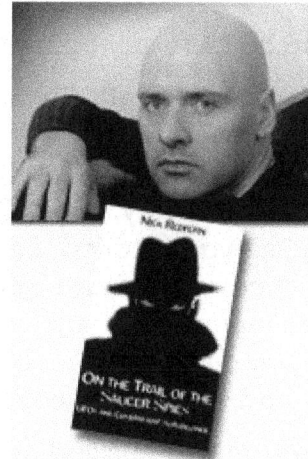
Britisher Nick Redfern and his own literary version of the MIB.

would come towards me quite quickly and appeared to increase in size, and then reversed and moved sideways at a middle speed. But it always returned to its original position just above the hills.

"Over an hour or so, the light gradually receded until it was just like a pin-prick of light. Well, I went to sleep, but the next night I wondered if it might be there again – and it was. This happened on a few occasions and I got quite used to seeing it when it was a clear night.

"To be honest, I got quite friendly with it, really. I didn't feel threatened by it, because although it came close to our farm, it didn't come that close. Now, when I'd seen it a few times, I decided that I would get a compass and graph paper and try to track where it was coming from because this was intriguing me. I thought, this is a bit different."

It was what happened when Henson approached officials that really set wheels in motion: "After I saw the light for a few times and tracked the movements of it, I contacted [Royal Air Force] Chivenor. I told them what I'd seen and then I got a letter saying that my sighting was being looked at. Then this chap turned up at the house.

"It was an evening when he arrived for the first time, and he pulled up in this old black car; and when he came in the house he was wearing a black suit and tie. I would imagine that he was in his late thirties and I was most disappointed that he wasn't wearing a uniform. He announced himself as a Royal Air Force official and, of course, I took it as such. To me, he was an authority, put it like that. He actually came to visit me on several occasions. I assumed he was from RAF Chivenor; he didn't actually say so. I was a bit over-awed that somebody was actually coming to see me.

"Altogether," Henson explained, "he came on three nights. On the first night he came up to my bedroom and we sat there waiting for the clouds to clear. Unfortunately, that night and the next night he came, we couldn't see anything. So, he said that he would have to come back again. Now, on the third night, he saw it."

Did he have any opinion as to what the phenomenon was?

"No, none at all, he was just concentrating on looking at it. But he was very cagey. He wasn't very friendly, but he wasn't nasty either. But on this night he took some photos of the light. He didn't seem very surprised by what he saw. It was all very, very low-key, which I suppose is the way to play it if it was something unusual. If he'd have got excited, I'd have got excited. He then left and he took his camera and took my compass drawings and notes – and I never got them back. But before going he said that nobody else would believe what I'd seen and there was no point in me talking about it at school. At that age, you don't want to be laughed at – and my family had laughed at me, anyway."

Henson was puzzled about her bizarre experience:

"I thought originally that it was some military object, but then the Ministry of Defense said it was a planet, although that didn't explain the way it moved. Now, it all hinges on whether or not you believe in UFOs. I can't see why there shouldn't be life on other planets. And if there is, why shouldn't they come here to have a look at us?"

Anne Henson's case is a classic Man in Black encounter. It started with the sighting of a strange object and was followed by a visit from a dark-suited authority figure who warned her not to talk about what she had seen, and who confiscated her compass drawings and notes that displayed the movements of the phenomenon she had observed. But Henson's account differs in one striking aspect to many other Men in Black accounts that remain unverifiable. The official files on her experience have now been officially declassified and they identify her mysterious, black-garbed visitor as an employee of the British Royal Air Force's elite Provost and Security Services – the equivalent of the United States' Air Force Office of Special Investigations (AFOSI).

That an organization of this caliber would take a keen interest in the subject of UFOs is intriguing to say the least. The Confidential report on Anne Henson's encounter that was prepared by Sergeant S.W. Scott of the P&SS's Special Investigation Section states:

"MISS ANNE HENSON, aged 16, said that on 30th August, 1962 between 10.30 p.m. and 10.55 p.m. she opened the window of her room which faces N.N.E. and saw a diminishing star-like object with what appeared to be red and green colored flames coming from it. It was slightly larger than the average star and appeared to be round. After about 21/2 minutes it became very small and she could only see it with the aid of binoculars. She was quite sure that it was not the navigation lights of an aircraft because she had seen these many times and could recognize them immediately.

"She did not look for it again until 17th October 1962, when she saw the object again which was partially obscured by fog. With the aid of binoculars she compared the object with several stars and noticed that the stars were silvery white whereas the object was red and green. Near to and above the object she noticed another exactly similar but smaller object. She noticed a difference in the color of the original object which was now emitting green and orange flames in the same way as before.

"MRS. C. HENSON, mother of ANNE HENSON, said that she had seen the object described by her daughter. She could offer no explanation as to the identity of the object but was of the opinion that it was not a star. She declined to make a written statement.

"A visit was made on 1st November, 1962 when the sky was clear and all stars visible. MISS HENSON, however, said that the object was not in view on this particular night. Observations were maintained for one hour but nothing was seen. MISS HENSON was asked to continue her observations and on the next occasion on which she saw the object or objects to compile a diagram showing its position in relation to the stars. This she agreed to do.

"On 28th November, 1962, the next available opportunity, [the witnesses address] was again visited. However, although observations were maintained for 2 hours the sky remained obscured and nothing was seen. MISS HENSON was interviewed and said that she had seen the objects again on two occasions and although she had compiled a diagram she had omitted to note the date. She said that she would again watch for the objects noting times and dates and compile another diagram which she will forward by post to this Headquarters.

"MISS HENSON reports unidentified aerial phenomena and provides a diagram showing their position in relation to stars. The objects have not been seen by the Investigator who cannot therefore give an opinion as to their identity. It is considered that MISS HENSON is a reasonable person, although at

16 years of age girls are inclined to be over-imaginative. However, MISS HENSON is supported by her mother, a person of about 50 years of age, who seems quite sincere. The matter should be brought to the notice of [the] Department at Air Ministry set up to investigate such phenomena."

Sergeant Scott's report was ultimately dispatched to an Air Intelligence office that concluded Anne Henson had simply misperceived a celestial body, such as a star or a planet, an explanation with which Henson vehemently disagrees. Whatever the truth of this curious affair, however, its importance in the field of MIB research cannot be stressed enough.

# ARE THE MIB KILLING OUR UFO RESEARCHERS? BY PROF. G. COPE SCHELLHORN

Sometimes the Men In Black become UFO Terrorists when they step over the line and become cold blooded killers. Prof G.C. Schellborn is a seasoned investigator in his own right having authored several best selling works, including ETs In Biblical Prophecy. His body of evidence is not very good for UFO researchers staying alive into their golden years. Many have died way before they should have as this investigative piece rightly brings out.

*　　*　　*　　*　　*

Death by gunshot to the head. Death by probable poisoning. Death by probable strangulation. Deaths possibly by implantation of deadly viruses. No one lives former. Yet the recent suspicious deaths of UFO investigators Phil Schneider, Ron Johnson, Con Routine, Ann Livingston and Karln Turner, as well as the deaths of a host of researchers in the past, only seem to add emphasis to a reality with which many of the more aware UFOIogists are now quite familiar: not only is UFO research potentially dangerous, but the life span of the average serious investigator falls far short of the national average.

Mysterious and suspicious deaths among UFO investigators arc nothing new. In 1971, the well-known author and researcher Otto Binder wrote an article for Saga magazine's Special UFO Report titled "Liquidation of the UFO Investigators:' Binder had researched the deaths of "no less than 137 flying saucer researchers, writers, scientists, and witnesses' who had died in the previous 10 years, "many under the most mysterious circumstances."

The selected cases Binder offered were loaded with a plethora of alleged heart attacks, suspicious cancers and what appears to be outright examples of murder. We will have occasion to refer to many of these cases, but first let us take a look at more recent evidence of highly suspect deaths among present day researchers.

## Phil Schneider

No one has shook up more those who have been following UFO fact and rumor the past low years than Phil Schneider. Schneider died January 17, 1996, reportedly strangled by a catheter found wrapped around his neck. If the circumstances of his death seem highly controversial, they are matched by the controversy over his public statements uttered recently before his death.

Phil Schneider was a self-taught geologist and explosive expert. Of the 129 deep underground facilities Schneider believed the U.S. government had constructed since World War II, he claimed to have worked on 13. Two of these bases were major, including the much rumored bioengineering facility at Dulce, N.M. At Dulce. Schneider maintained, "grey" - humanoid extraterrestrials worked side by side with American technicians. In 1979, a misunderstanding arose. In the ensuing shootout, 66 Secret Service, FBI and Black Berets were killed along with an unspecified number of "greys. It was here he received a beam-weapon blast to the chest which caused his later cancer.

If Schneider is telling the truth, he obviously broke the code of imposed silence to which all major black-budget personnel are subjected. The penalty for that misstep is presumably termination.

Schneider in fact maintained that numerous previous attempts had been made on his life, including the removal of lug nuts from one of the front wheels of his automobile. He had stated publicly he was a marked man and did not expect to live long.

Some of Schneider's more major accusations are worthy of attention:

Phil Schneider was found murdered was involved in top secret UFO work when he met his fate.

(1) The American government concluded a treaty with "grey" aliens in 1954. This mutual cooperation pack is called the Grenada Treaty.

(2) The space shuttle has been shuttling in special metals. A vacuum atmosphere is needed for the rending of these special alloys, thus the push for a large space station.

(3) Much of our stealth aircraft technology was developed by back-engineering crashed ET craft.

(4) AIDS was a population control virus invented by the National Ordinance Laboratory, Chicago, Illionois.

(5) Unbeknownst to just about everyone, our government has an earthquake device: The Kobe quake had no pulse wave; the 1989 San Francisco quake had no pulse wave.

(6) The World Trade Center bomb blast and the Oklahoma City blast were achieved using small nuclear devices. The melting and pitting of the concrete and the extrusion of metal supporting rods indicated this. (Remember, Schneider's forte, he claimed, was explosives.)

Finally, Phil Schneider lamented that the democracy he loved no longer existed. We had become instead a technocracy ruled by a shadow government intent on imposing their own view of things on all of us, whether we like it or not. He believed I l of his best friends had been murdered in the last 22 years, eight of whom had been officially disposed of as suicides.

Whatever we think of Phil Schneider's claims, there is no denying that he was of peculiar interest to the FBI and CIA. According to his widow, intelligence agents thoroughly searched the premises shortly after his death and made off with at least a third of the family photographs.

THE ALIEN DIGEST

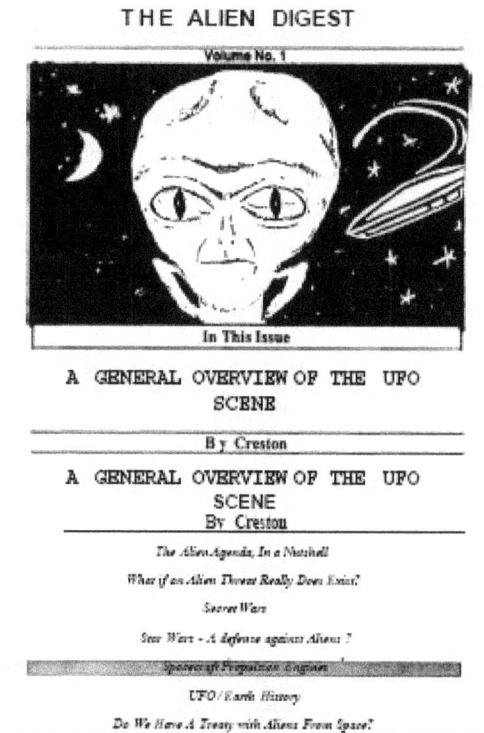

Volume No. 1

In This Issue

A GENERAL OVERVIEW OF THE UFO SCENE

By Creston

A GENERAL OVERVIEW OF THE UFO SCENE
By Creston

*The Alien Agenda, In a Nutshell*

*What if an Alien Threat Really Does Exist?*

*Secret Wars*

*Star Wars - A defense against Aliens ?*

*Spacecraft Propulsion Engines*

*UFO/Earth History*

*Do We Have A Treaty with Aliens From Space?*

Though not a professional looking publication, Ron Rummel did seemingly manage to include material in his Alien Digest that pissed someone off.

## Ron Rummel

Another recent disturbing case is the death of Ron Rummel, ex-air force intelligence agent and publisher of the Alien Digest, on August 6, 1993. Rummel allegedly shot himself in the mouth with a pistol. Friends say, however, that no blood was found on the pistol barrel and the handle of the weapon was free of fingerprints. Also, according to information now circulating, the suicide note left by the deceased was written by a left-handed person. Rummel was right-handed. Perspiration on the body smelled like sodium pentothal, or so it is alleged.

The Alien Digest ran to seven limited issues, all now almost impossible to acquire. One thing is certain. Ron Rummel's magazine was touching on sensitive issues such as the predator/prey aspect of the alien/human relationship and the use of humans as food and recyclable body parts. Did Rummel cross a forbidden line? It would seem so. But which line, and where? Interestingly enough, one of Rummel's friends was Phil Schneider, and the two had been collaborating.

## Ron Johnson

An equally disturbing and more recent death is that of Ron (Jerrold) Johnson, at the time MUFON's Deputy Director of Investigations. Johnson was 43 years old and, it would seem, in excellent health. He had just passed a recent physical examination with the proverbial flying colors. However, on June 9, 1994, while attending a Society of Scientific Exploration meeting in Austin, Texas, Johnson died quickly and amid very strange circumstances. During a slide show, several people sitting close to him heard a gasp. When the lights were turned back on, Johnson was slumped over in his chair, his face purple, blood oozing from his nose. A soda can, from which he had been sipping, was sitting on the chair next to him.

Did Ron Johnson die of a stroke? Possibly. An allergic reaction? Another possibility.

Some of the more outstanding facts of Ron Johnson's life might easily lead a more skeptical-minded person to a tentative conclusion that his death was probably neither accidental nor natural. For instance, his most recent job was with the Institute of Advanced Studies, purportedly working on UFO propulsion systems. He had been formerly employed by Earth Tech, Inc., a private Austin, Texas, think tank headed by Harold Puthoff. It would appear he held high security clearances, traveled frequently between San Antonio and White Sands, and had attended 2 secret NATO meetings in the last year or so. One of those meetings, it is rumored dealt with ET communications.

Although advanced in years, there are some who believe that Dr. Hynek's death was because of "strange circumstances," due to the high number of researchers who have died of brain tumors or cancer.

If all or most of the facts offered above are accurate, one thing seems obvious: Johnson was walking both sides of the street. This in itself was highly dangerous, and he may have paid the ultimate price in an attempt to serve more than one master.

As for exactly what killed Ron Johnson, a number of possibilities beyond natural ones present themselves. It is quite easy in this day and age to induce strokes through chemicals or pulsed radiation. It is just as easy, and has been for some time, to induce heart attacks and other physical debilitations, such as fast-acting cancers. The best bet is that Ron Johnson was eliminated by a quick-acting toxin, perhaps a nerve agent. As for exactly why he was killed, we will probably never know. The autopsy, somewhat ludicrously, has been officially classified as inconclusive.

# Ann Livingston

As a side note, a nurse returning home from Austin shortly after Johnson's death reported a similar death-situation aboard her plane. When she tried to move rearward to offer her assistance, she was forcefully restrained from doing so. Could it be, one wonders, that some agent, through an accident, was the victim of his own machinations? The idea strikes a nice note of poetic justice, if in fact that were the scenario.

Another death involving elements of high strangeness is that of Ann Livingston, who died in early 1994 of a fast-form of ovarian cancer. Livingston made her living as an accountant, but she was also a MUFON investigator and had in fact, published an article entitled "Electronic Harassment and Alien Abductions" in the November 1993 MUFON Journal. The article was highly critical of Julianne McKinney, director of the Electronic Surveillance Project of the Association of National Security Alumni. McKinney discounts U FO phenomena, believing that what passes for such is most often one kind of governmental ploy or another, whether in the form of experimental machinery or experimental psychology.

Some facts which seem relevant to the case stand out. At 7:15 AM, December 29th 1992, Livingston's apartment close to O'Hare airport, in Chicago, Illinois, was lit up brightly by a silver white flash. She was accosted later in the day while in her apartment parking lot by 5 MIBs (Men in Black) which she described as being almost faceless and carrying long, flashlight-like black objects. She was rendered unconscious. What, we must ask, assuming her story is true, was done to her at this time, and why'? And did it have anything to do with her later rapidly-advancing ovarian cancer?

It is not a well-known fact that Ann Livingston had been previously abducted. Her friend, Fran Heiser, has stated that Ann Livingston had met two handsome people, a man and woman, on an earlier trip to Mexico. To Livingston's surprise, the man told her that the attractive young lady she was meeting was in fact her daughter.

# Karla Turner

Could genital intrusions from past UFO abductions have poisoned in some way Ann Livingston's system? That is exactly the suspicion Karla Turner (author of Maquerade of Angels, Taken, and Into the Fringe) had about the breast cancer that preceded her death during the summer of 1996. Both publicly and privately, Karla Turner held up the specter of alien retaliation for statements she made in print, especially in Masquerade of Angels. How much her suspicions were founded in reality we will probably never know. (Her husband has made al her books available for free at http://www.karlaturner.org/)

Who or what is killing UFO investigators now and in the past? Probably some of the deaths presented here-that look at first glance so suspicious---are in fact natural or accidental or self-inflicted because of stress or mental imbalances. But, as Otto Binder noted more than 25 years ago, there are so many. Pure common sense, and good logic, should lead us to believe that the high incidence of premature death in a field which has a limited number of investigators is very disproportionate compared to the population at large.

Spider Web of Causes

What we may have IS a concatenation, a spider web, of interweaving threads which are causal and often, in fact, deadly. One thread is the activities of the US (and other) intelligence agencies. Another thread is possible ET involvement. A third thread is the involvement of certain PSI-tech think tanks and private PSI/PK practitioners, including negative occultists. A possible fourth thread is highly reactionary religious cults which feel they are carrying out the will of God. It is more than likely that one or more or all of the above agencies are responsible in whole or in part for many of the deaths from the recent past, which have already been mentioned and many of those remaining cases from the present to the more distant past, some of which we will now explore.

# Danny Casolaro

Danny Casolaro, an investigative reporter looking into the theft of Project Promise software, a program capable of tracking down anyone anywhere in the world, died in 1991, a reported suicide.

Casolaro was also investigating several UFO "NO-Nos" Pine Gap, Area 51 and governmental bioengineering.

# Mae Bussell

Not long ago, Mae Bussell, a gutsy, no-holds-barred, investigative radio host died of a fast-acting cancer just like Ann Livingston and Karla Turner. Bussell was acutely interested in UFOlogy.

The directors of APRO, Coral and Jim Lorenzen, a Tucson-based UFO group, both died of Cancer.

# Deck Slayton

Deck Slayton, the astronaut, was purportedly ready to talk about his UFO experiences, but cancer also intervened.

# Brian Lynch

Brian Lynch, young psychic and contactee, died in 1985, purportedly of a drug overdose. According to Lynch's sister, Geraldine, Brian was approached approximately a year before his death by an intelligence operative working for an Austin, Texas, PSI-tech company. Geraldine said they told Brian they were experimenting on psychic warfare techniques. After his death, a note in his personal effects was found with the words "Five million from Pentagon for Project Scanate."

At the time of his death Elkins was deep into the study of the Ra Material, a lengthy and complex series of channeled teachings that had begun in January 1981 and which he had been researching with Carla Rueckert and James McCarty. There are reports of negative psychological interferences having developed during this latter investigation.

# Capt. Don Elkin

In the '80s Eastern Airlines pilot Capt. Don Elkin committed suicide. He had been investigating the UFO coverup for over 10 years and, at the time, was deep into the study of the Ra material with Carla Rueckert. There are reports of negative psychological interferences having developed during this latter investigation.

# Bizarre Death of Scientists

Certainly nothing is stranger, and breeds speculation more quickly, than the 30-some-odd deaths associated with SDI (Star Wars) research at Marconi Ltd. in England between approximately 1985-1988. Here in capsulated form is a list of a few of the more bizarre deaths:

Roger Hill, a designer at Marconi Defense Systems, allegedly commits suicide with a shotgun, March 1985.

Jonathan Walsh, a digital communications expert employed by GEC, Marconi's parent firm, falls from his hotel room, November 1985, after expressing fear for his life.

Ashad Sharif, another Marconi scientist, reportedly tied a rope around his neck, and then to a tree, in October 1986, got behind the wheel of his car and stepped on the gas with predictable results.

In March of 1988, Trevor Knight, also associated with Marconi, died of carbon monoxide poisoning in his car.

Peter Ferry, marketing director of the firm, was found shocked to death with electrical leads in his mouth (August 1988).

Also during the same month of the same year, Alistair Beckham was found shocked to death with electric leads attached to his body and his mouth stuffed with a handkerchief. He was an engineer with the allied firm of Plessey Defense Systems.

And, finally, but by no means the sole remaining death in this unique cluster, Andrew Hall was found dead in September of 1988 of carbon monoxide poisoning.

What, you may be asking, does SDI research have to do with the deaths of UFO investigators? Theoretically, quite a lot. If, as many investigators have hypothesized, Star Wars research was initiated with the dual purpose of protecting "us" against Soviet aggression and/or the presence of UFO craft in our atmosphere, then several possibilities arise. Most compelling is the idea that the soviet KGB, realizing that the Western powers were on the verge of perfecting a high-powered beam-weapon that could be used from outer space or atmospheric space against them, marshaled a last-gasp, all-out espionage offensive to slow or destroy the project. If this scenario is true, and the weapon was indeed successfully developed, we have an explanation for the collapse of the Soviet Union ("Surrender or you might be incinerated").

Other explanations have been offered. For example, scientists working on the project discovered the true nature of the research they were involved with and the overwhelming stress led them to suicide. Or they discovered that their real collaborators were "greys," or Western politicians working with/for grey aliens. One thing seems obvious. Something went terribly wrong at Marconi. Scientists usually don't commit the kinds of bizarre, "unscientific" suicides we find here.

One other possibility is that a contingent of unfriendly ETs got wind of what GEC and Marconi and its affiliates were up to and, to protect themselves, created enough psychic trauma within the minds of many of the scientists to drive them to suicide. But if this is so, why have the deaths stopped? Has the project been shelved? Highly unlikely. The best bet is that the project was completed, roughly about 1988, and whatever it is, beam-weapon or otherwise, it is now operational.

Certainly neither the public at large, and not even UFOlogists generally, seem thoroughly aware of the real risks UFO investigators run. In fact those UFOlogists who are aware of the suspicious deaths of some of their colleagues in the 50s and 60s, seem to believe that whatever forces and agencies that were then responsible have softened their tactics in the `80s and `90s. The evidence, as we have indicated, does not seem to support such a conclusion. There is no doubt, however, that the `50s and `60s produced some strange goings-on.

# Jessup and McDonald

Undoubtedly the most intriguing (and perhaps appalling) deaths in UFOlogy were those of Dorothy Kilgallen, M.K. Jessup and Dr. James McDonald - the former an alleged accident, the latter two purported suicides. The details of these deaths, despite official pronouncements to the contrary, are disturbing to say the least. Each of the three individuals seemed to have much to live for, all were successful, and everyone of them was deeply immersed in the relatively new UFO-phenomena problem.

## Dorothy Kilgallen

Dorothy Kilgallen was the most famous syndicated woman journalist of her day. Stationed in England in 1954 - 55, and privy to the highest levels of English society and its secrets, she wired two unusual dispatches which may have contributed to her death. The first, sent in February 1954, mentioned a "special hush-hush meeting of the world's military heads" scheduled to take place the following summer. The 1955 dispatch, which barely preceded her death from an alleged overdose of sleeping pills and alcohol (a la Marilyn Monroe), quoted an unnamed British official of cabinet rank, `We believe, on the basis of our inquiry thus far, that saucers were staffed by small men-probably under four feet tall. It's frightening, but there is no denying the flying saucers come from another planet.'

Dead girls tell no tales. Blond bombshell Marilyn Monroe may have been involved with various characters from MJ12 while gossip columnist Dorothy Kilgallen was also into data dealing with crashed UFOs.

Whatever the source (rumored to be the Earl of Mountbatten), this kind of leak in the atmosphere of the mid- 50s was an unacceptable leak. It is well to recall that the secret CIA-orchestrated Robertson Panel had met in 1953 and issued the Robertson Report. Briefly summarized, this document-and the attitudes reflected there - represented a new hard-line attitude to covering up all significant UFO phenomena. The year 1953 and the meeting of the Robertson Panel truly initiated the UFO cover up as we know it today, with a few extra dollops having been added.

Did Dorothy Kilgallen actually commit accidental suicide? There appears to be an excellent chance she had help.

# Dr. James McDonald

Dr. James McDonald, senior physicist, Institute of Atmospheric Physics and also professor in the Department of Meteorology at the University of Arizona, died in 1971 purportedly of a gunshot wound to the head. There is no one who had worked harder in the 60s than McDonald to convince Congress to hold serious, substantial subcommittee meetings to explore the UFO reality of which he was thoroughly convinced. He was definitely a thorn in the side of those who maintained the official cover up and, needless to say, his passing to them would be a blessing.

McDonald, allegedly depressed, shot himself in the head. But, alas, he didn't die. He was wheelchair-ridden but somehow, several months after his first attempt, he allegedly got in an automobile, drove to a pawnshop, purchased another pistol from his wheelchair, drove to the desert and did himself in. How convenient, one might say, for his adversaries. And McDonald, there can be no doubt, had made enemies. The question is: How much did these enemies aid and abet the demise of this most worthy and influential campaigner?

# Astronomer M.K Jessup

When astronomer and archaeologist M. K. Jessup allegedly committed suicide in Dade County Park, FL., in 1959 certain alarm bells should have gone off. There is no doubt the well-known author of such influential works as The Case for the UFO and The Expanding Case for the UFO had been depressed. Things had not been going well for him, and he had, it must be admitted, indicated his gloom to close friends, Ivan Sanderson, the biologist, and Long John Nebel, the well-known New York City radio host. Sanderson reported him disturbed by "a series of strange events" which put him "into a completely insane world of unreality."

The author of Case For The UFO, Dr M.K. Jessup took his own life under a set of mysterious circumstances.

Was the reality Jessup was faced with at the time "completely insane" or were there, perhaps, forces driving Jessup to the edge, forces with a plan? Anna Genzlinger thoroughly investigated his death. Her conclusion: "He was under some sort of control." Remember, these were the days of secret governmental mind-control experiments which have only recently been uncovered.

Certain facts about the case raise red flags. For example, no autopsy was performed, contrary to the state law. Sergeant Obenclain, who was on the scene shortly after Jessup's body was discovered, has said for the record, "Everything seemed too professional." The hose from the car exhaust was wired on; and it was, strangely, washing machine hose. Jessup died at rush hour, with more than the usual amount of traffic passing by. He had been visited by Carlos Allende three days before his death and according to his wife, had been receiving strange phone calls.

We know the navy was very much interested in what he was doing; and we all know, or should know, it is the ONI (Office of Naval Investigations) that has been in the forefront, from the very beginning, of the UFO coverup.

And what of particular interest was Jessup investigating at the time? Something that was top secret and would remain so for some time: the Philadelphia Experiment.

Dr. James McDonald tried to convince Congress to look into the UFO situation. He died after shooting himself a short while later.

The late astronomer Dr. M.K. Jessup was the first to reveal details of the Philadelphia Experiment-he died a few months later.

# Frank Edwards

Frank Edwards, the noted news commentator, died of an alleged heart attack on June 24, 1967, on the 20th anniversary of the Kenneth Arnold sighting. Was that coincidence?

Probably not. Several other prominent UFOlogists died the same day, Arthur Bryant, the contactee, Richard Church, chairman of CIGIUFO and the space writer, Willie Ley. The circumstances surrounding the death of Edwards, who like James McDonald was pushing for meaningful Congressional subcommittee meetings, raise huge questions. It so happens that a "World UFO Conference" was being held in New York City at the Commodore hotel on that very day in June, chaired by UFO publisher and author Gray Barker. Barker stated publicly that he had received two letters and a telephone call threatening that Frank Edwards, who was not in attendance, would not be alive by the conference's end.

It definitely looks like someone was sending a message. As an unhappy sequel to this account, Rep. Rouse, who had been supporting Edwards in his campaign for Congressional attention to the UFO issue, died of a similar heart attack shortly afterwards.

The annals of UFOlogy are frighteningly filled with the deaths of UFOlogists from unusual cancers, heart attacks, questionable suicides and all manner of strange happenings. Did former Secretary of Defense James Forrestal really commit suicide as purported by jumping out a hotel window at about the time saucers may have been crashing down in the southwestern desert? Was UFO writer Damon Runyon, Jr.'s suicidal plunge off a Washington D.C. bridge in 1988 really an act of will? What really happened to Dr. B. Noel Opan who, in 1959, after an alleged visit by MIBs, disappeared, as did Edgar Jarrold, the Australian UFOlogist, in 1960.

How do we explain the rash of heart attacks that took so many: Frank Edwards, Rep. Rouse, author H. T. Wilkins, Henry E Kock, publicity director of the Universal Research Society of America, author Frank Scully and contactee George Adamski? How do we correlate accurately the large number of purported suicides, including: Rev. Della Larson, contactee, author Gloria Lee (Byrd), Marie Ford, UFO enthusiast who discovered Larson's body, researcher Doug Hancock, and, more recently, researcher Feron Hicks? What do we do with the inordinately large number of cancer deaths which pepper the UFO field and burn doubtful holes in our credulity: Canadian researcher Wilbert B. Smith, Brazilian researcher Dr. Olavo Fontes, Jim and Coral Lorenzen (photos are earlier in this article), and the deaths of biologist Ivan Sanderson and CUFOS founder James A. Hynek (photo at the start of this article) (both from rare brain cancer)?

Certainly not all of these individuals, as well as many other less prominent researchers that space limitations do not allow us to mention, were marked for termination. Many, perhaps most, died natural deaths. But so many of the cases leave doubt; some seem to be branded by the mark of Cain. We know now how easy it is to induce strokes and heart attacks through chemicals, pulsed beams and microbes. We have learned that the federal government was (and still is) involved in PSI-tech research. An individual's mind is rather easily manipulated, and minds can be subtly beaten like putty into despair and madness.

# Jvan T. Sanderson

The late Ivan T. Sanderson passed away unexpectedly. He was head of a major UFO/paranormal group!

The late Ivan T. Sanderson passed away unexpectedly. He was head of a major UFO/paranormal group!

UFOlogy is not the safe, hobbyist pastime some would like it to be. There is danger, real danger in sticking your nose in places where the powers that be don't want you to be. Many of the deaths related above are highly suspicious. Some appear to be outright murder.

What is the cause, who the villain? Again, it must be emphasized that the "problem" is complex. Rogue intelligence agencies, negative ET groups, freelancing PSI-tech firms, and reactionary cultist groups all seem to play, or to have played, a part in the more nefarious UFO-related events described here including the possible homicides of UFO researchers in past decades as well as more recently. It seems highly likely that sometimes one or more of these agencies may be working together, either with or without the knowledge of the other's presence.

What can we do about such a state of affairs? Several things. We can inform ourselves like good democratic citizens. And we can inform others. We can and must raise a hue and cry when we suspect foul play. If we are to protect our very lives and the democratic hopes we say we cherish, then we must not go, silent and ignorant, into the night, pretending an innocence we have not earned.

## THE ALIEN DIGEST

Volume No. 3

In This Issue

### MORE NOTES ON THE UFO SCENE

**By Creston**

The Alien Crash at Roswell 7/2/1947
Current Abductions and Genetic Experiments
Orion and the Unholy Six
Richard Shaver's View of the Grays
MJ12 Wars and Military Preparedness
What Aliens Don't Want You to Know
Invisible UFOs
More on the Reptoids
Dr. Edward Teller's Anti Gravity Research
Hitler's Fourth Reich
The Dragon People
Bigfoot
The Greatx 1934 Alien-Human War at Tucson Arizona
Space Settlement Project
Radio Electronic Combat

And more...

# THE MYSTERIOUS LIFE AND DEATH OF PHILIP SCHNEIDER BY TIM SWARTZ WITH ASSISTANCE FROM CYNTHIA DRAYER

Al Pratt suspected something was wrong with his friend Philip Schneider. For several days in a row, Al had gone to Phil's apartment, in Willsonville, Oregon, saw his car in the parking lot, but received no answer at the door. Finally, on January 17th, 1996, Al Pratt, along with the manager of the Autumn Park Apartments and a detective from the Clackamas County Sheriff's office entered the apartment. Inside, they found the body of Philip Schneider. Apparently he had been dead for five to seven days. The Clackamas County Coroner's office initially attributed Philip Schneider's death to a stroke. However, in the following days disturbing details about his death began to surface, leading some to believe that Philip Schneider had not died from a stroke, but had in fact been murdered.

Philip Schneider's life was certainly as controversial as his death. He was born on April 23, 1947 at Bethesda Navy Hospital. Philip's parents were Oscar and Sally Schneider. Oscar Schneider was a Captain in the United States Navy, worked in nuclear medicine and helped design the first nuclear submarines. Captain Schneider was also part of OPERATION CROSSROADS, which was responsible for the testing of nuclear weapons in the Pacific AT Bikini Island. In a lecture videotaped in May 1996, Philip Schneider claimed that his father, Captain Oscar Schneider, was also involved with the infamous "Philadelphia Experiment." In addition, Philip claimed to be an ex-government structural engineer who was involved in building underground military bases (DUMB) around the country, and to be one of only three people to survive the 1979 incident between the alien Grays and U.S. military forces at the Dulce underground base. Philip Schneider's ex-wife, Cynthia Drayer believes that Philip was murdered because he publicly revealed the truth about the U.S. government's involvement with UFOs.

For two years prior to his death, Philip Schneider had been on a lecture tour talking about government cover-ups, black budgets, and UFOs. Philip stated in his lecture that in 1954, under the Eisenhower administration, the federal government decided to circumvent the Constitution and form a treaty with extraterrestrials. The treaty was called the 1954 Greada Treaty. Officials agreed that for extraterrestrial technology, the Grays could test their implanting techniques on select citizens. However, the extraterrestrials had to inform the government just who had been abducted and subject to implants. Slowly over time, the aliens altered the bargain, abducting and implanting thousands of people without reporting back to the government.

In 1979, Philip was employed by Morrison-Knudsen, Inc. He was involved in building an addition to the deep underground military base at Dulce, New Mexico. The project at that time had drilled four holes in the desert that were to be linked together with tunnels. Philip's job was to go down the holes, check the rock samples, and recommend the explosives to deal with the particular rock. In the process, the workers accidentally opened a large artificial cavern, a secret base for the aliens known as Grays. In the panic that occurred, sixty-seven workers and military personnel were killed, with Philip Schneider being one of only three people to survive. Philip claimed that scars on his chest were caused by his being struck by an alien weapon that would later result in cancer due to the radiation.

If Philip Schneider's claims are true, then his knowledge of the secret government, UFOs and other information kept from the public, could have serious repercussions to the world as we know it. In his lectures, Philip spoke on such topics as the Space-Defense-Initiative, black helicopters, railroad cars built with shackles to contain political prisoners, the World Trade Center bombing, and the secret black budget.

Quotes taken from a lecture given by Philip Schneider in May, 1995, at Post Falls, Idaho.

# Railroad Cars

"Recently, I knew someone who lived near where I live in Portland, Oregon. He worked at Gunderson Steel Fabrication, where they make railroad cars. Now, I knew this fellow for the better part of 30 years, and he was kind of a quiet type. He came in to see me one day excited, and he told me 'they're building prisoner cars.' He was nervous. Gunderson, he said, had a contract with the federal government to build 107,200 full length railroad cars, each with 143 pairs of shackles. There are 11 sub-contractors in this giant project. Supposedly, Gunderson got over 2 billion dollars for the contract. Bethlehem Steel and other steel outfits are involved. He showed me one of the cars in the rail yards in North Portland. He was right. If you multiply 107,200 times 143 times 11, you come up with about 15,000,000. This is probably the number of people who disagree with the federal government. "

## "Star Wars" And The Alien Threat"

"68% of the military budget is directly or indirectly affected by the black budget. "Star Wars" relies heavily upon stealth weaponry. By the way, none of the stealth program would have been available if we had not taken apart crashed alien disks. None of it. Some of you might ask what the space shuttle is 'shuttling." Large ingots of special metals that are milled in space and cannot be produced on the surface of the Earth. They need the near vacuum of outer space to produce them. We are not even being told anything close to the truth. I believe our government officials have sold us down the drain - lock, stock and barrel. Up until several weeks ago, I was employed by the U.S. government with a Rhyolite-38 clearance factor - one of the highest in the world. I believe the "Star Wars" program is there solely to act as a buffer to prevent alien attack - it has nothing to do with the 'cold war,' which was only a toy to garner money from all the people. For what? The whole lie was planed and executed for the last 75 years."

## Black Helicopters

"There are over 64,000 black helicopters in the United States. For every hour that goes by, there is one being built. Is this the proper use of our money? What does the federal government need 64,000 tactical helicopters for, if they are not trying to enslave us. I doubt if the entire military needs 64,000 worldwide. There are 157 F-117A stealth aircraft loaded with LIDAR and computer-enhanced imaging radar. They can see you walking from room to room when they fly over your house. They see objects in the house from the air with a variation limit of one inch to 30,000 miles. That's how accurate that is. I worked in the federal government for a long time, and I know exactly how they handle their business."

## Terrorist Bombings

"I was hired not too long ago to do a report on the World Trade Center Bombing. I was hired because I know about the 90 some odd varieties of chemical explosives. I looked at the pictures taken right after the blast. The concrete was puddled and melted. The steel and the rebar was literally extruded up to six feet longer than its original length. There is only one weapon that can do that - a small nuclear weapon. A construction-type nuclear device. Obviously, when they say that it was a nitrate explosive that did the damage, they're lying 100 percent folks. I want to further mention that with the last explosion in Oklahoma City, they are saying that it was a nitrate or fertilizer bomb that did it. " First, they came out and said it was a 1,000 pound fertilizer bomb. Then, it was 1,500. then, 2,000 pounds. Now its 20,000. You can't put 20,000 pounds of fertilizer in a Rider Truck. Now, I've never mixed explosives, per se. I know the chemical structure and the application of construction explosives. My reputation was based on it. I helped hollow out more than 13 deep underground military bases in the United States. I worked on the Malta project in West Germany, in Spain and in Italy. I can tell you from experience that a nitrate explosion would have hardly shattered the windows of the federal building in

Oklahoma City. It would have killed a few people and knocked part of the facing off the building, but it would have never have done that kind of damage. I believe I have been lied to, and I am not taking it any longer, so I'm telling you that I have been lied to."

In 1987 Philip married Cynthia Marie Drayer Simon. The two had met in June of 1986 at a meeting of the Oregon Agate and Mineral Society. As Cynthia put it years later, "He had so many interesting stories, so much information to share, we bonded and love began to bloom." Philip and Cynthia would later have a daughter, Marie Schneider. Unfortunately their marriage had difficulties. According to Cynthia, health problems contributed to their break up. Philip had multiple health concerns, many of which could have killed him. He had chronic lower back pain that never went away, even after a back operation. He had multiple Sclerosis, which was chronic and progressive. Occasionally he had to use, crutches, a body brace, leg braces, bladder bag, catheter, diapers, and a wheelchair. He often had to sleep in a hospital bed with railings, a helmet, and body braces. When Cynthia first met him he was taking Dilantin for seizures, and almost died 3 times from this medication due to an allergic reaction.

Philip also had Brittle Bone Syndrome (osteoporosis) and cancer in his arms. He had hundreds of shrapnel wounds, a plate in his head with a metal fragment in his brain, fingers missing from his left hand. There was a scar that ran down from the top of his throat to below his belly button, and another scar that ran from just under his ribs, side to side. Cynthia would later state " Philip was a complex person. he had brain damage after a bomb was dropped on him while working as a civilian structural engineer for Morrison-Knudsen in Vietnam. He had a Rhyolite clearance. He was learning disabled, brilliant in some areas, yet unable to fill out a form in the Doctors office. Able to create time travel formulas, but unable to budget money; he had to file bankruptcy one year. I now believe that he had been 'deprogrammed' so that he could not remember most of his 'past' life. But something began to happen shortly after we first met. Perhaps because of the seizures, or because he changed his medication, or because he now had another person to talk to that was interested in what he had to say, he began to remember the old days. Being the scientific, logical minded person I am, I listened intently to his stories with a grain of salt, waiting for additional information to verify them. I can still remember the night he began to talk in some foreign language (sounded like Chinese and another night in what sounded like French.) Philip told me he knew 11 languages before the brain damage. After the space shuttle, Challenger, exploded, I visited Philip in his apartment. He had a large chalk board with complicated formulas which proved that a 'cosmosphere' had shot down the space shuttle."

Cynthia also said, "It was a difficult marriage for both of us, which was complicated by a failed self-employed business selling rocks, minerals, and antiques, Philip's re-constructive surgery on scars on his chest, his lower back operation, my gall-bladder surgery and the birth of our daughter, all within a 1 year period. The pressures of our new family, failed business, and physical problems culminated in our divorce in 1990. Philip was an emotional abuser and could be very mean and abusive. He was a complex person - part genius and part paranoid schizophrenic. We had a bad marriage but developed it into a great friendship."

One of Philip's more amazing stories was his fathers alleged involvement with the "Philadelphia Experiment." When Philip's father, Captain Oscar Schneider (Navy Medical Corp.) died in 1993, Philip discovered original letters in his basement. According to Philip, the letters were evidence that the Philadelphia Experiment actually existed, and that Oscar Schneider had been a participant in it after the crew members had been quarantined in a Virginia psychiatric ward. Captain Schneider supposedly autopsied the bodies of the crew members as they died, and found alien implants in their arms, legs, behind their eyes, and deep inside their brains. Captain Schneider was confused by these implants, so they obviously were not military. They had to have been alien in nature, and the small "transistor" like item was discovered before transistors had been invented. Here was evidence that either by accident, or on purpose, aliens were involved with the Philadelphia Experiment, and were probably responsible for its failure.

Also discovered in Oscar's basement were photographs taken during Operation Crossroads, in which a nuclear device was used on Bikini Island. Authentic military photos taken from an airplane showed UFOs raising up from the lagoon and flying through the mushroom cloud. These photos however, mysteriously disappeared from Philips apartment at the time of his death.

Some investigators in Philip Schneider's mysterious death have had problems believing some of the incredible claims he made before he died. Even those who knew Philip when he was alive didn't always accept the validity of his stories. Cynthia Schneider noted that when Philip was under crisis or pressure, he would tell people that he had been arrested, or that people from the sheriff's office or government had been at his door. This was the way he expressed his crisis. Unfortunately she claims, sometimes it was true, Like "the little boy who cried wolf," his friends became numb to his reports.

Despite the fact that Philip's claims seemed too wild or disturbing to be true, he obviously believed in what he was saying. Philip claimed that his life was in danger because he was revealing the truth, a truth that some would kill to keep secret. He borrowed a gun from his friend Ron Utella, stating that he felt he needed protection and that there had been several attempts to have his car run off the road. In the end, though, Philip's safeguards were not enough to save his life. On either January 10 or 11, 1996, Philip Schneider died under mysterious circumstances.

After the initial cause of Philip's death was listed as a stroke, Cynthia asked to see the body before it was to be prepared for cremation. She was dissuaded by the funeral director who felt that the body's advanced state of decomposition would be too traumatic. However, she could not shake the feeling that something was wrong. The next day Cynthia was contacted by Detective Randy Harris who said that "something was wrong" - that there were marks on Philip's neck. Philip Schneider's body was removed from the funeral home and autopsied by Dr. Karen Gunson, Medical Examiner for Multnomah County, Oregon. The autopsy revealed that Philip had in fact died as a result of having a rubber hose wrapped three times, tightly around his neck and tied in a knot. The conclusion from the autopsy was that he had committed suicide. He had wrapped the tubing around his neck, tied it in a knot, blocked the flow of blood to his head, became unconscious and finally died.

More surprising was Cynthia's discovery that Philips lecture material, unknown metals, military photographs, and all notes for his unwritten book on UFOs were missing from his apartment. However, money and other valuables were left untouched.

When he was found in his apartment, Philip's body was in an unusual position. His feet were under the bed, his head was in a wheelchair seat, at an unusual angle, the rest of his body was on the floor, hands by his sides. There was blood found on the floor near the wheelchair, but no blood was found on the wheelchair. There were no apparent wounds on Philip's body to account for the blood. No sample of the blood was taken due to the initial belief that Philip had died of natural causes. No suicide note has ever been found. In fact, Mark Rufener, a long time friend of Philip said, " I saw Philip the weekend of January 6 and 7th 1996. We were going to buy land in Colorado. We were excited because he was going to hire me to help write a book about his knowledge on UFOs and aliens, the One World Government, and the Black Budget. He did not commit suicide, he was murdered and it was made to look like a suicide. "

When he was alive, Philip enjoyed eating out at the 76 Truck Stop in Aurora, Oregon. A waitress named Donna remembered his stops when they would talk about his work. Philip mentioned to her that there had been 19 attempts to stop him from talking. Donna states that Philip said "If they ever say that I have committed suicide, you will know that I have been murdered." She said that Philip believed he had a mission to talk about a government cover-up about aliens and UFOs, and that there were forces out to stop people who talked.

Was Philip Schneider murdered? His ex-wife Cynthia believes this to be the case. She thinks that Philip was met by someone he knew and injected with a drug in order TO incapacitate him. The assailants then wrapped the rubber hose around his neck, asphyxiating him. In fact, shortly after Philip's death, several friends told Cynthia that they had seen Philip with an unknown blond women several weeks before he died. During the course of the meeting, Cynthia noticed a long-haired blond women in a car, watching the meeting through the window with a pair of binoculars. When they tried to approach the car, the woman quickly sped away. Cynthia later traced the license plate number and it turned out to be from a truck, with the plate reported as stolen. Cynthia thinks the reports of women with blond hair is significant because Cynthia's mother, through a channeling session, had told her that a woman wearing a blond wig was involved in Philip's death.

Despite the fact that officials have closed the case as a suicide, and Philip's surviving siblings have tried to persuade Cynthia to accept the ruling, Cynthia has not stopped in her efforts to discover the truth in her ex-husband's death. She says that she knows in her heart and soul that Philip would not have committed suicide willingly, and she still hopes that Philips blood and urine can be relocated by the Multnomah County Medical Examiner's Office and examined for traces of drugs that would not normally be there. However, as the days go by the reality for such tests grows smaller. She still hopes that someone will come forward with pertinent information to help her find justice for Philip's death. Until that time comes, Cynthia Drayer will continue her task, perhaps putting her own safety at risk. That prospect doesn't frighten her anymore, " I just want people to know the truth about Philip Schneider, a person who died trying to expose the difficult truths of this world."

If you have any information concerning the death of
Philip Schneider, you can E-mail Cynthia Drayer at: cimbid@aol.com

Phil Schneider

## Something Looks Strange My Friend
## Compiled By Robert Goreman

On January 9, 1967, Mr. Edward and Mrs. Arline Christiansen and family returned home after a trip to Florida to their new house in Wildwood, New Jersey. A UFO sighting made the previous November was the last thing on their minds.

At 5:30 PM, there was a knock at the door.

A representative of the "Missing Heirs Bureau" said that he was looking for an Edward Christiansen who had inherited a great deal of money. This investigator dressed in black and stood at least six-foot-six with an enormous frame, with thyroid eyes, dead white skin, and pipe-stem limbs. His shoes featured unusually thick rubber soles. Despite his size, the visitor spoke in a high "tinny" voice that issued in an emotionless monotone, in clipped phrases, "like a computer." When he removed his jacket, he disclosed an official-looking gold badge on his shirt pocket which he instantly covered with his hand and removed.

As he sought personal information to determine if he had located the missing heir, this investigator wheezed with labored breathing and his face got redder by the minute. He asked for a glass of water and swallowed a large yellow pill. He returned to normal after taking it.

Arline and her seventeen-year- old daughter Connie both noticed that the inquisitor's too-short trousers had ridden up his skinny leg and saw a thick green wire that came out of his sock and disappeared under his pants. The wire seemed to be indented into his leg at one point and was covered by a large brown spot.

Although UFOs were never mentioned, this case is pure MIB.

When the visitor left the house and reached the road, he gave a hand signal and a 1963 black Cadillac pulled alongside with its headlights out. The stranger climbed into the car and it drove off, its headlights still off.

# ABDUCTION RESEARCHER KARLA TURNER THE MEN IN KHAKI BY GREG BISHOP

UFO Mystic.com

The 1994 MUFON convention featured one speaker whose book I had read and who I wanted to speak with. Fortunately, I had an excuse for an interview because of a zine I was publishing at the time.

The researcher was female, a rarity in the UFO field. She had written two books on the abduction scenario, *Into The Fringe*, and *Taken*, which impressed me as different views on the subject than were making the rounds at the time. There was little discussion of breeding programs or alien takeover of our genetic material. Instead, she examined what the phenomenon meant to the individuals involved, on a personal as well as a symbolic level.

It was with a little nervousness that I introduced myself to Karla Turner. She turned out to be a polite, charming, and intelligent person, although I don't know why I expected otherwise. Perhaps it was the forthright tone in her writing, which conveyed a strong dedication and no-nonsense attitude.

She agreed to an interview, which we conducted at the hotel in Austin where the convention was held. At this point, I was willing to accept most of the abduction stories as true, at least as many of the witnesses reported them. I still have little doubt that Turner was sincere and honest about her experiences, and those of her husband, who had both been subject to strange visitations for many years. She didn't really care about people who questioned her interests and tended to ignore all but those who could offer useful information in her quest for answers.

The interview was published, and Turner took me seriously enough to keep up a correspondence for two more years, until her death in 1996. We talked on the phone once every month or two, and she suggested people and subjects that I might want to study. Most of them had little or nothing to do with abductions.

Strangely, almost every piece of mail that I received from Turner showed evidence of tampering. Some were simply left open, while others were sealed in plastic with an apology from the US Post Office. I asked her about this, and she began to send envelopes with a piece of tape over the flap, writing "sealed by sender" over it. The tampering stopped. This sort of thing happened with only one other person, and he was a cattle mutilation researcher.

One experience made me wonder about not just Turner herself, but the whole subject of abductions in general. On the night before our interview, I woke up four or five times: at 1:11, 2:22, 3:33, etc. This is the only time this has happened in my life. Turner and others later told me that this was a little-known experience of many who had claimed anomalous interludes with the UFO phenomenon. My host in Austin, Wes Nations, told me that his neighbors had seen people in khaki outfits looking around his home the day after I left, and that a fire had broken out soon after they disappeared. It did little damage, and may have been a coincidence, but made all of us wonder just what it was that Karla Turner had uncovered.

Listen to Greg Bishop every Sunday night at
www. RadioMisterioso.com

# THE GUARDIAN
# MEN IN BLACK, AN INVESTIGATION
# SUBJECT BOB OECHSLER

Among the attachments included here are responses to questions submitted regarding CURSE.TXT, Guardian, "Original Guardian", Alien Liaison book reference authored by Timothy Good, etc. and the following file listings.

[1] Biographical Information Sheet - Bob Oechsler

[2] Guardian Investigation - UFO Video Case (February 1993)

[3] Insider's Report - Investigating the Guardian Enigma

The latter is an in depth report on the investigation through May of 1993. There have been other interesting revelations and discoveries since then that again tend to support more of Guardian's claims reported as "preposterous" by Robert Stack on the "Unsolved Mysteries" broadcast of 2-03-93. My personal experience indicates that this one case has been subjected to more diversified scientific scrutiny than any other UFO case. Much of that is no doubt due to the fact that there exists such an abundance of tangible evidence to work with, both tactile and corporeal. With that stated, I'll start by responding to the questions in order of number received.

1) Unspecified Guardian question ... (Lee)

[RES] ... Refer to attached [2] & [3] above.

2) Was Bob approached by an MIB? ... (Leslie)

[RES] ... While I have researched the MIB (Men In Black) phenomenon for several years and recently investigated a possible MIB incident in Maryland, I cannot confirm that I've ever been directly approached by anyone or anything fitting the common description. Suggested reading: The UFO Silencers, Mystery of the Men In Black authored by Timothy Green Beckley, Inner Light Publications 1990 New Brunswick, NJ.

3) Was Bob's house broken into & was a (tape) stolen? (Leslie)

[RES] ... There has never been any evidence of my house being "broken into". However, there was an incident in 1989 during the course of several field investigation trips to Gulf Breeze, Florida wherein several audio taped interviews and two very important computer disks mysteriously vanished from my somewhat less than perfectly organized home office. I should point out that we did find overt evidence of mail tampering between myself and Ed Walters including undelivered packages of photographic and mapping materials. The evidence was submitted to postal authorities and an investigation initiated which stopped the illegal practice at least for six months.

4) Did Bob ever meet with the Guardian? What did he learn? (Dave)

[RES] ... In November of 1992 while on location shooting part of the "Unsolved Mysteries" segment with the Cosgrove-Meurer Production Company, we received a telephone call at our hotel in Kanata, Ontario from an individual who professed to know the identity of Guardian. I stayed an extra day after shooting just to meet with this individual who was providing numerous contact names, addresses and phone numbers for corroboration including that of the individual he claimed was Guardian.

The person that I met with was a local college student who had known Guardian for 17 years and claimed to be long time friends. He reported an incident where his friend had shown the Guardian video tape along with other tapes, documents and photographs to a group of six people including himself. The incident was fresh in his mind because he thought all of this UFO stuff was nonsense and he remembers falling on the kitchen floor laughing in hysteria. His friend was so adamant about the veracity and authenticity of the material that he assured him that he was the Guardian and that it was all true. It wasn't until he heard and saw local news reports of eyewitnesses to the events and that NBC was in town filming that he realized there may be more to it than he first thought.

I called the number he gave me for the Guardian and tried to arrange a meeting by leaving a message on an answering machine. Guardian called his friend back and left a message for me on his machine basically denying any knowledge or complicity. The more the friend challenged him, the more remote he became. However during the course of my investigation it became abundantly evident that this individual was in fact the Guardian of whom I was searching. Only forensic evidence is yet to be collected for final proof. Nonetheless I an quite convinced that I know who Guardian is and an awful lot about him and the events hr has been involved in for many years. I never believed it was necessary to expose him because all of the other witnesses and landing contamination effects was sufficient. to validate the case. The bottom line is simply that not one of Guardian's rather outrageous claims has been disproved and quite a number of them have so far been completely validated.

5) Is the Guardian the same one as "original guardian" described in CURSE.TXT? ... (Peter)

[RES] ... A review of CURSE.TXT reveals that "original guardian" referenced is an executive with the motion picture. My suspect is clearly not involved in that field. The so called "incident" occurred in a city east of Toronto, that is a rather large area. The video taped landing incident that I investigated occurred about 30 miles west of Ottawa, which is some 200 miles east of Toronto. The Guardian involved in the case I investigated was clever enough to put his fingerprint on the label of video tapes he sent out. That makes them unique in as much as it certainly cuts down on Guardian claimants and that's why we featured that issue on the "Unsolved Mysteries" and "Sightings" segments. The Guardian documents that I investigated referred to a roll of 35mm film of alien images that was submitted by an anonymous photographer to NRC (National Research Council) in Ottawa. We have not to date been able to verify if such a roll of film was received at that repository, but it does seem to coincide to a certain degree with the "original guardian" reference. In summary, there does appear to be some possible similarity in the two cases but there is insufficient detail in the CURSE.TXT report that I have to draw even the slightest parallel or even to determine if there exists a mergence of the two. It is difficult to give much credence to reports that are warranted by unsigned individuals and even more difficult to find rationale to prompt research and investigation.

6) Was Bob ever taken to an off-shore research platform by the Gov't and shown an anti-gravity chamber? ... (Mike)

[RES] ... As reported in the hardback book Alien Liaison - The Ultimate Secret authored by Timothy Good and originally published by Random Century Ltd, London 1991 (47 weeks on the London Times Best Seller List) and subsequently in paperback by Arrow Books Ltd, London 1992 and now available in the U.S. under the title Alien Contact published by William Morrow Company, NY 1993, the chapter called Cosmic Journey refers to a project which I was involved in under commercial secrecy contract to Kenneth Feld Productions Special Development Group out of Orlando, Florida. The project was sanctioned by the White House Office of the National Space Council and by NASA (National Aeronautics and Space Administration), the latter of which I was a former employee during the mid-seventies. I was retained for the project due to my robotics expertise and involvement in the adaptation of the manipulator arm for the Shuttle Project as well as my expertise in innovation of RF remote control systems, and all of that not withstanding my UFO research credentials.

The activities referred to in the question relate directly to my involvement with a former astronaut and Air Force General Officer in the U.S. Intelligence establishment at the Pentagon. On a project trip to the Houston area, I was taken along with a group that filled three unique helicopters to a NORAD (North American Defense Command) facility located on an off-shore platform off the Gulf Coast between Mobile, Alabama and Pensacola, Florida. We were flown from Ellington and were on the platform little more than an hour at most. Refer to one of the above books for details. During the same visit to the Houston area I visited a facility southwest of Houston referred to as the Micro-Gravity Research Center. It did not involve to my knowledge the swimming pool facility which I believe is located at the Johnson Center complex and did not involve the famous airplane retro gravity airborne project. This facility housed a micro-gravity chamber which was encompassed in a room approximately 20' x 40' and housed several dozen if not hundreds of experiments, protein crystal experiments being one of the most notable to me. A small scale model of the manipulator arm on the shuttle was previously arranged and set-up for me along with a computer simulation for modeling modifications. The purpose of my visit was to install design changes with limiter stops and axis weight changes for adaptation to a gravity environment for the full scale model for the Cosmic Journey Project. I believe the micro-gravity environment was effected by an unusual lighting system installed in the ceiling. The effect was analogous to what it might be like if one could stand inside a florescent light tube. For more information, again refer to the above referenced books.

7) Was the space tracking station (off-shore research. platform) on the "fence" off the SC coast? ... (Peter)

[RES] ... The facility was not on the Atlantic Seaboard, see question six above for location. I am not familiar with the reference "fence". The off-shore facility was not to my knowledge a research center. It was an on-line NORAD monitoring facility with capabilities far exceeding ordinary space tracking.

8) What was Bob's position at NASA? What does (position) mean? ... (Mike)

[RES] ... My NASA credentials are referenced in the book Alien Update authored by Timothy Good and published in the U.K. et.al. by Arrow Books Ltd 1993. The photo section depicts my original NASA identification photo badge with security number in black and white, the original is in color. My position was titled Mission Specialist which is a catch all reference given to about half of the employees at the Goddard Space Flight Center, the rest were referred to as Operations Specialists. My job entailed project engineering, documentation and sub-mission appraisal. Some of the projects that I worked on included the Apollo-Soyuz Test Project (docking collar latch mechanism), the IUE (International Ultraviolet Explorer), the manipulator arm connecting mechanism for the Shuttle Project and several DOD (Department of Defense) missions. I had no interest or knowledge of the UFO phenomenon during my tenure at NASA and have repeatedly announced my failure to recognize the connection to my work at NASA and my subsequent UFO research other than as it has applied to the Cosmic Journey Project. I continue to be amazed at the wild conspiracy theories and the constant speculation about my supposedly working as some kind of a mole for the Gov't. My position has always been that if the Gov't doesn't know what UFO researchers have discovered, then they ought to know and probably do know a great deal more than all of the researchers combined.

9) I'm still wondering how he managed to go from doing freelance research (under NASA auspices) on some video tapes taken by a contractor to being able to order a military polygraph for a Canadian official that was allegedly taken against her/his will aboard an ET craft, ... (Bob Perse)

[RES] ... Since you're wondering, perhaps I can shed some light on the issues for you. Actually I prefer interested individuals to ask this sort of question rather than blindly speculate. First let me clarify the "freelance research on some video tapes" issue. As a video and photographic analyst, I was very interested in the depiction at close range of a UFO craft in flight shot by Ed Walters in Gulf Breeze, Florida on December 28, 1987. The moving images afforded an opportunity to evaluate the fundamental operational physics of the craft and since I had been cited by the United States Chamber of Commerce for my work in field applications technologies in robotics there existed a natural interest in determining the prospects of the video taped object being a remote controlled model. Therefore I was asked by several groups including "Unsolved Mysteries" and the Fund for UFO Research to have a look at it. I was looking for an independent lab where I could conduct my analysis in privacy and without commercial expense. Since I have several former associates still working at GSFC (Goddard Space Flight Center) within thirty minutes of my home, including the local MUFON (Mutual UFO Network) director of investigations, it was natural to inquire of the possibility of conducting my work in their rather well equipped studios during off-peak hours. Arrangements were made with the section director at GSFC TV Studios to move the necessary equipment into one of their editing studios. There was no official inquiry on the part of NASA HQ nor GSFC hierarchy since the station which is closed circuit was operated by Bendix. Therefore the work I was doing was clearly NOT under the "auspices" (look it up) of NASA.

The second and independent issue which does not appear connected in any way that I can imagine relates to the Guardian Case. The Canadian Official initially contacted me anonymously by mail, but included enough information that I was able to locate the individual due to my knowledge of the landing area. The individual claimed to be having explicit memories relating to the landing event depicted on the "Unsolved Mysteries" broadcast. I did not learn until later that this individual had significant credentials within the Canadian Government. The claims involved witnessing the landing event, being taken onboard the craft and interacting with not only the alien entities depicted on the program but also a human being of a specific nationality as being in charge of the operation involving the craft and entities. There was never any allegation regarding being taken against anyone's will since no invitation was extended or refused.

The issue involving the taking of a polygraph examination of the claims was raised due to the sensitivity of the witness' position within the Canadian Government. Since the witness was not acting on behalf of any agency of the Canadian Government and the onboard events did not directly involve same (in other words the witness was not onboard as a representative of the Canadian Government), there existed a need for specific anonymity in order to avoid the appearance of a potential international incident. For clarification it should be noted that the witness' voice and/or likeness would be readily recognized at any Canadian Embassy throughout the world. Therefore in order to establish credibility for the claims of an anonymous witness, it was clear to all interested parties that a polygraph exam of the witness claims would be required for the record to be included as a valid contribution to an already complex case. I did not order a military polygraph, I selected a polygraph examiner in Canada who had been trained by the U.S. Military. Dr. Bruce S. Maccabee (Ph.D. Optical Physics and Exec. Dir. of FUFOR) assisted me and the polygraph examiner in developing the questionnaire strategy in consultation with skeptic Jerry Black who arranged the polygraph for Travis Walton, Allen Dallas, etc. just before the 1993 release of "Fire in the Sky". We wanted to be sure that any positive polygraph result could not only be supported, but subjected to review by other examiners.

It seems to me that this last question poses some important points that should serve these inquires well. We need to be very careful about jumping to conclusions. It does not seem fair to me that just because someone exercises care and diligence in investigative technique, that somehow this correlates with heavy handed old fashioned CIA tactics. Or somehow suggests that the analyst or investigator is secretively entrenched in some covert government plot. I do recognize that conspiracies have and do exist, but my experience suggests that such activity is vastly overstated in UFO research activities. It's really not needed here as most researchers in this field tend to bicker and debate so much that precious little actual research ever gets accomplished much less accepted. When it comes to establishing public opinion the tabloids win hands down it seems simply because they are so well financed.

Hope this proves helpful and doesn't bore anyone to tears. Thanks very much for the questions. I believe the Guardian Case will eventually make for a good book and could serve as an excellent template for future investigations of this nature. If you think writing a book is going to make anyone rich, I suggest you try getting something published. It always amazes me when skeptics try using the old rich and famous explanation to attempt to discredit witnesses and researchers/investigators. It is quite a naive ploy in the eyes of the informed.

Thanks again,
Cheers.
BoB Oechsler

# Biographical Information Sheet - Bob Oechsler

## BoB Oechsler: Pronounced X-ler

Former NASA Mission Specialist
Goddard Space Flight Center
Greenbelt, Maryland
Who's Who Listings
Who's Who in the East
Who's Who in Finance and Industry
Who's Who in the World
International Book of Honour
Author - The Chesapeake Connection
Contributing Author: The Gulf Breeze Sightings - Walters
Wm. Morrow, New York 1990
* Alien Liaison - Good
Random Century LTD, London 1991
The DFO Report 1992 - Edited: Good
Sidgwick & Jackson, London 1991
Alien Contact - Good
Wm. Morrow, New York 1994
Alien Update - Good
Arrow, Random House, London 1994

Bob Oechsler got out of the UFO field shortly after he got waylaid by a mysterious character known as The Guardian.

* 27 weeks on the London Times Best Seller List.

Lecturer: The Franklin Institute, Philadelphia

Speaker: The United States Chamber of Commerce

International Television exposure:

NBC - "Unsolved Mysteries" (Regular Consultant)

ABC - "America's Best Kept Secrets"

ABC News - With Science Editor Jules Bergman

CBS - "UFOs: The Best Evidence" (Award Winning Documentary)

FOX - "Sightings"

Syndicated - "Now It Can Be Told"

Central Television - London

BBC - London

NTV - Tokyo, Japan

RAI - Rome, Italy

META - Berlin, Germany

Technical Expertise: Photo & Video Analysis

Invented process for converting nighttime Polaroid images into almost daylight conditions for easy analysis.

Professional Expertise: Robotics Field Applications Technologies

Electro-gravitics Research

Radio & Television Broadcasting

Primary Guidance within the U.S. Intelligence Community:

Central Intelligence Agency (CIA) - Science & Technology

U S. Naval Intelligence - Director, Naval Ops Air Warfare

National Security Agency (NSA), Institute of Def. Analysis

Defense Intelligence Agency (DIA)

Executive Branch - Defense Science Board

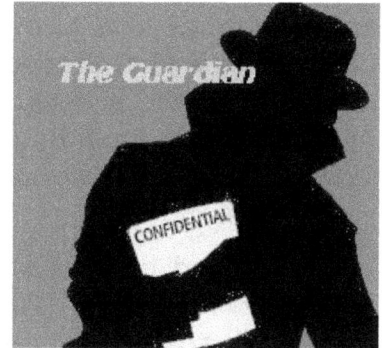

It didn't take brain surgery for Bob Oechsler to get caught up in the intrigue surrounding the Men In Black.

# Guardian Investigation – The UFO Video Case

## February 1993

The Ottawa, Ontario UFO Landing reported by the anonymous Guardian has resulted in a year long active field investigation. I believe it to be a landmark case which involved the complete cooperation of several agencies in Canada including the Department of National Defence. DND has participated actively in the investigation to the extent of providing an alert team ready to respond to any continued helicopter harassment activity at the site and witness residence. Although we have interviewed several witnesses to this helicopter activity, we have yet to identify the perpetrators in spite of several photographs taken at times of intrusion.

Transport Canada has been quite cooperative in providing classified radar data at the site location. The National Research Council has been receptive to my investigation of Guardian claims, classified helicopter research activity and has provided access to CSIS, the Canadian Secret Intelligence classified radar data at the site location. The National Research Council has been receptive to my investigation of Guardian claims, classified helicopter research activity and has provided access to CSIS, the Canadian Secret Intelligence Service. Energy, Mines and Resources have provided aerial photography for the research area. Canadian UFO author Arthur Bray and researcher Graham Lightfoot have provided invaluable assistance in the investigation. CUFORN, the Canadian UFO Research Network has been helpful in providing me with a background on Guardian's prior UFO report for 1989 and original materials they received from Guardian including photographs and video tape.

Scheduled broadcasts of the investigation by network television include NBC's "Unsolved Mysteries" (February 3rd) and Fox's "Sightings" (February 12th) clearly achieve Guardian's implied interest in widespread exposure for alien UFO activity in the Ottawa Valley area. Television attention of this caliber should give significant credit to the investigation and open the door for those reluctant to come forward for fear of ridicule. These broadcast provide the first international exposure for this case which centers around the events instead of the anonymous Guardian who video taped the extraordinary landing event.

Guardian began reporting UFO incidents in the area where the landing occurred as far back as November of 1989. The landing was video taped without the knowledge of other witnesses to the event on August 18, 1991. We discovered the landing site and witnesses on May 10, 1992 and began an investigation based on contamination evidence suggesting an extraordinary event which affected the site. I have testimony of several experts in diversified scientific fields which strongly argues against human technological involvement in the event.

The size of the craft was approximately 20-25 feet in diameter as determined by correlating field tests. The flares or Pyrotechnic activity at the site has been determined to be of unknown origin, not compatible with any universally known compounds. The craft depicted in the video apparently left residue elements identified as not being indigenous to the site. Acoustics analysis of the video tape correlates with the geography and particular topography of the investigated field site. A Fast Fourier Transform (FFT) from a Digital Audio Tape (DAT) taken from an original Guardian supplied copy of the video detailed no evidence of electrical fields, repeating pulses or oscillations within the detection frequency range of the recording equipment used, yet all ambient sounds typical to the scenario depicted in the video including the distant sounds of barking dogs, wind noise, insects, camera operator breath walking as well as camera equipment noise in close proximity to the microphone were all identifiable. No unknown is could be attributed to the object or pyrotechnics depicted in the video.

NBC invested in excess of $115,000 unsuccessfully attempting to duplicate the effects in the Guardian video and concluded that to fake what was observed in the video would have taken a sizeable investment and would have been virtually impossible to Pull off without the cooperation of the residents in the neighborhood, some of whom have agreed to polygraph examination in order to refute that possibility. Even NASA's JPL was unable to find evidence of hoaxing the event depicted in the video.

After five research and investigation trips to Canada, the task is not yet complete. The final conclusions may only be reached upon meeting the anonymous Guardian who holds the keys and answers to many questions. The single most important question that remains to be answered is: "How did Guardian know that the craft was going to land at that time and place?".

My remaining efforts will be focused on establishing a dialogue with Guardian. His decision to remain anonymous is in my opinion prudent. Removing public anonymity can only put the dialogue with Guardian. His decision to remain anonymous is in my opinion prudent. Removing public anonymity can only put the focus on his credibility and integrity instead of the incredible event itself. My objective will be to encourage his cooperation upon confirming his identity and ascertain the rationale to his methodology and determine the level of veracity of his claims.

BoB Oechsler

# The Insiders Report
# By Bob Oechsler

## Investigating The Guardian Enigma

### NBC's "Unsolved Mysteries" airs video of landed UFO craft.

### FOX's "Sightings" features this landmark UFO landing case.

A strange series of events unfolded during the summer of 1991 in a rural area about 20 miles west of Ottawa in the Ontario Province of Eastern Canada. Out of the rolling hills and heavily wooded swamp lands of West Carleton Township, residents were reporting surrealistic screams, excruciating cries of tormented agony that warned off all attempts by residents to investigate. Those that went to the edge of the forest land to look into the matter were met not only with silence at first, but an eerie permeating sensation of fear that seemed to hang over the area. The strange silence was penetrated by a startling scream like no other sound experienced before. Even the dogs would not venture into the area as their keen senses warded them off ahead of their inquisitive masters. This was but one of a pattern of unusual events that rained down on this sparsely populated residential former farming estate community that summer. One individual now known publicly as Guardian had the courage to investigate and report his unique findings of unusual activity.

Guardian began reporting in late 1989 to UFO research organizations in Canada that American and Canadian Security Agencies were engaged in a conspiracy of silence. He anonymously claimed that UFO sightings in the Ontario region had intensified in the 1980's (specifically around nuclear power generating stations) and that on November 4, 1989 Canadian Defense (sic) Department radars picked up a globe shaped object traveling at a phenomenal speed over Carp, Ontario. The UFO, Guardian reported, abruptly stopped and dropped like a stone. He claimed that the ship landed in deep swamp in a rural area of West Carleton Twp. While monitoring satellites traced the movements of the alien occupants, two AH-64 Apache choppers and a UH-60 Blackhawk helicopter descended on the area the following night. Guardian says they carried full weapon loads and were part of a covert American unit that specialized in the recovery of alien craft. Independent UFO investigations revealed no less than three eye witnesses confirming the hovering craft over the swamp area, sounds of explosions, military vehicles and personnel with no identification marks blocking off a main access road to the swamp area. Guardian reported the recovery of "three reptilian fetus headed beings" listed as Class I NTEs (Non Terrestrial Entities) identified as muscular, grey-white skinned humanoids.

Guardian's rather elaborate report details a matrixed dielectric magnesium alloy craft driven by pulsed electromagnetic fields generated by a cold fusion reactor. He reveals that the craft was of a military nature and coldly calculates a mission designed to pit human species against human species in an ideological war to further strain east-west relations. His expressed knowledge of alien installed human implants, military operations, high technology EMP (Electro-Magnetic Pulse) weapons and ELF (Extremely Low Frequency) waves calibrated to the same wavelength as the human brain to subliminally control test subjects all suggest an extraordinary intimate involvement in these events. If his assertions are correct, then we humans are in for a tough time regardless of the official secrecy surrounding these issues. Guardian warns of an impending hostile invasion much like the concerns expressed numerous times by former President Ronald Reagan about a potential "Force from outer space". He reports that data aboard the recovered sphere explains why the aliens are so comfortable on our world. They preceded humans on the evolutionary scale by millions of years and that their civilization was destroyed 65 million years ago during an interdimensional war forcing them to leave the earth. Now they have chosen to attempt to reclaim what was once theirs.

Guardian was not the only one to report evidence of UFOs and alien entities in the township of West Carleton. Alana Masters (pseudonym) reported to the local press in September 1989 that her daughter had been making drawings of a ghost with big black eyes and spoke of unusual dreams and visitors at night. One evening before retiring, Alana was drawn to a winnow looking out over her back yard by a bright light. Concerned about the unusual shape of the object idling silently out back, she went to check on her two and a half year old daughter. Upon opening the door she was startled to see two beings that had really dark eyes and glowed a whitish yellow color. One of the entities turned toward Alana and the next thing she remembered was waking up on the sofa the next morning. Alana's neighbor reported seeing a glowing creature of like description appearing to be taking ground samples from the back yard and another in her house. She said she never would have mentioned the event were it not for Alana's report. The Canadian

National Research Council reported over 100 UFO sightings reports during the same period.

In February of 1992 a video tape and several constructed documents arrived at my mailbox postmarked from Ottawa, Ontario. There was no return address, but the video tape was cleverly labeled with the name Guardian accompanied by an inked finger- print as a unique identifying reference. The documents contained a map of the same area as reported in the 1989 UFO landing event, but referenced a newer landing and retrieval occurring on August 18, 1991. The cover document was fabricated with a DND Department of National Defence) stencil, a maple leaf watermark and two photocopies of Polaroid flash pictures depicting events in the video. Other documents resembled typical FOIA (Freedom of Information Act) responses involving deleted classified data using a black "magic" marker. The documents contained the same ideology referred to in Guardian's 1989 report, but seemed to focus more on theology and Nostrodamus type apocalyptic proclamations. Had it not been for the exceptional video tape Guardian's reports would have no doubt been dismissed as the ravings of a misguided ideologist.

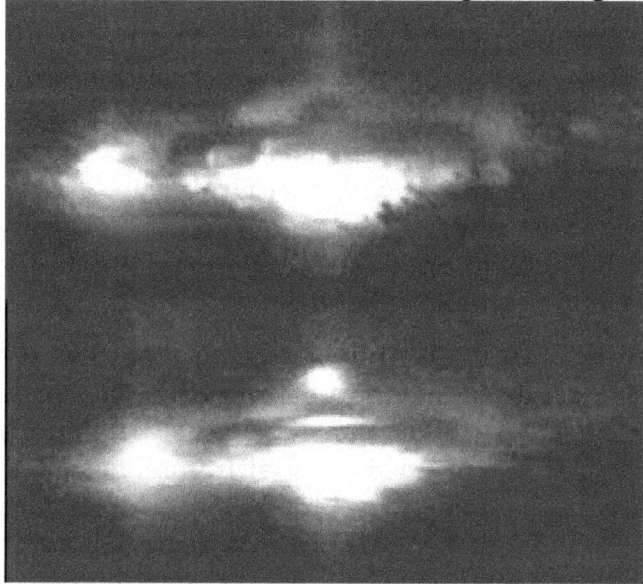

A video containing images of a supposed landed UFO on Canadian soil just called for Bob Oechsler to investigate.

Psychologists that I consulted reviewed the material and concluded that while there is evidence of pathology (perhaps sociopath) as it relates to the source's interpretation and explanation of the scenario, there exists no evidence of schizophrenia or other similar disorders. Guardian is clearly literate in some areas of ufology, but may lack the ability to discriminate extremist and conspiracy theorists viewpoints from traditional rationalists.

In April of 1992, I completed a preliminary video analysis on the case. The video appears to be a series of edited takes from a longer video. This was determined as a result of several stops and starts with the observance of technical changes in the setting. For example in earlier sequences there appear to be several flares burning with billowing smoke rising from that general area, in later sequences it appears that the flares had burned out yet the remnants of smoke are still visible. The individual segments may however just be a product of starting and stopping the camera in order to conserve battery power. Guardian may have missed the initial landing due to late arrival. If he was influenced by the intelligence aboard the craft, he may have been affected in such a way as to inhibit filming of the departure of the object.

The first segment that I examined depicts a wide angle nighttime field of view with a series of bright red fires or flares burning on the left side of the screen with smoke billowing up and to the right of the frame reference and an elliptical bright white light to the right of the frame on an approximate horizontal even plane with respect to the red lights. The luminosity of the flare activity is great enough to expose a tree line or forest area in the background not far from the luminous source. The segment depicts a variation of zooms in and out of the scene with slight panning action to the right and left. At the fully zoomed setting the camera is far enough away from the total scene so that both the left scene and right scene are still simultaneously visible, except during gross panning of the camera. The right side scene with the elliptical white light also exhibits a flashing blue strobe light vertically aligned above the primary light source. Residual light smearing is evident below and slightly bleeding to the right of both primary scenes. On the left scene the smear is red and on the right the smear is green with a central blue. This is typical of nighttime electronic photography and eyewitness reports typically confirm that smear color is reflective of the actual naked eye color observed in the prime light source. This segment runs 2 minutes and 20 seconds.

The second segment commences with the photographer walking closer to the scene of the strobing lights, apparently at the full zoomed in setting or perhaps the view that exhibits only the flashing lights is such that the actual disc is initially obstructed by the terrain horizon on approach. During the initial frames smoke is visible which is apparently luminated by light from below the frame horizon. The smoke continues to be visible throughout the segment. Through a series of zoom sequences, apparently while the photographer is still walking, a clear image of what appears to be a disc shaped object is visible especially when examined frame by frame. There appears to be two flares or red colored fires at the left front leading edge of the disc but at least separated from the disc which does not appear to be damaged or on fire.

The center of the top of the disc builds into a triangular shape or turret area. The flashing lights depicted in the previous segment resolve to a blue strobe that is oscillating about the outer portion of the top of the turret and each flash reflects off of the curved portion of the top side of the disc below. The strobe sequence is approximately 7.5 flashes per second and rotates vertically as opposed to typical horizontal strobes on emergency vehicles and aircraft. The luminosity intensity characteristics of the strobe are variable with high intensity flashes followed sequentially by low intensity flashes. On occasion during single frame analysis a square flash of light could be observed as the source of the strobe. On at least one frame it is conclusive that a squared light pattern was observed sourcing from amidships the turret area as opposed to the top of the turret and well above the area of observed reflection.

Additional features apparent in this segment include a series of vertical slats, appendages or ridges that appear on the outside of the disc equidistant from each other. These features are luminated by the plasmatic like light source emanating from the underside of the craft. It would be easy for the casual observer to view these features as windows or square porthole like features due to the shadowing effect caused by the distortion of light distribution as a result of the protrusion of the vertical slats around the disc's leading edge.

Another observed anomaly in this segment involves what appears to be a secondary moving strobe seen at times well above the primary strobing light. This is probably a product of the electronics in the form of a continuous ghost roll of the strobe that constantly repeats itself strobing from the bottom of the frame to the top much like a horizontal roll characteristic. It maintains a constant vertical alignment to the strobe and is consistent with experiments conducted using a vertical strobe. The segment runs for forty seconds.

The third segment depicts the disc at an intermediate distance without change in zoom reference. There is still evidence of flares burning near the left front of the disc. It is the most significant segment for measuring the strobe frequency characteristics. As a side reference, an interesting correlation exists between the 7.5 strobe frequency in this video and the 7.5 oscillation observed in the video of a flying craft taken in Gulf Breeze, Florida in December 1987. It should be noted that a tripod is never used by the photographer. All segments are hand held and attention is not always given to the viewfinder for frame referencing. This segment shows no evidence of the signal flares depicted in the first segment so it is not possible to develop an actual chronology regarding these segment sequences. The segment runs for two minutes and seven seconds.

The forth segment proved to be more of a challenge to analyze. The segment commences with a close-up hand held shaky view of the upper strobe area without depicting the reflection area on the top side of the disc surface. It depicts a disembodied rising strobe feature which we were able to duplicate in laboratory tests. As the segment unfolds, it appears that the photographer is walking toward a crest in topography exposing the full disc with strobing features at a wide angle much the same as in segment two, absent the back- lighting effects of the luminated drifting smoke from the pyrotechnics activity. The photographer then zooms in closer to expose previously observed details of the disc and immediate surrounding terrain. It appears that the two flares at the front left of the disc have burned out, assuming the photographer's orientation to the disc is similar to previous segments. This segment runs for one minute and six seconds.

Additional segments on the source video depict a variety of freeze frames related to the final close-up frames of the disc where a blue beam of light was apparently aimed directly at the camera from the disc itself. The tracking quality for most of the segment is quite poor. The bulk of the subject matter appears to relate to images of either photographs or actual video frames of an alien entity(s) of the generically typical gray (grey) variety with almond shaped black eyes. The facial features contain a dominant protrusion or snout which an eyewitness described as "pig nosed". Sequential images show one eyelid closing and other changes in facial features. The entity(s) appear to be self luminating as no external light source is evident capable of luminating the hands and facial features. Guardian sent one researcher an 8 x 10 black and white print of such a creature posed in the terrain depicted by the Polaroid prints with the foreground luminated by flash. These final segments run just over 26 minutes duration.

In order to estimate the actual distance of the disc from the camera, I conducted a field test using only Sony CCD 4 Lux 8x Zoom video camera. A 1000 foot course was laid out at 100 foot intervals. I then recorded wide angle and zoom variations of an ordinary highway road flare in like nighttime conditions to that of the source video. The comparative results suggested that the disc shaped craft in the source video, at it's closest point, would be approximately 500 to 700 feet from the camera assuming an object of 50 feet in diameter. A 25 foot diameter craft would place the camera at 1000 to 1200 feet at closest approach. The latter proved to be the most viable following a field investigation which located the site where the video was taken.

It was immediately apparent when comparing the nighttime video sequences from both cameras that the source video was taken with a field production quality camera probably costing tens of thousands of dollars. The color retention is extraordinary even from the perspective of my own personal experience with broadcast quality field production camera systems. Considering the ultra high luminosity characteristics of the bright white light emanating from the bottom of the disc structure, it is surprising that the camera was able to retain the red coloring of the flares. The flares or flare mix in pots are exhibiting a significant amount of smoke giving indications of an active localized thermal environment with a wind velocity and direction that would later prove consistent with meteorological reports for the date and time period reported. My tests with ordinary road flares did not exhibit the same amount of smoke, nor did my camera retain the red color as that of the source camera. Test conclusions tend to validate that a high technology camera was used and that the pyrotechnics were no less than military grade.

## Preliminary Conclusions

### (Prior to Field Investigation)

The evidence suggests the depiction of a real event. It can not be determined at this time whether the source is providing credible information relative to the depicted events in the video tape. Nonetheless I am convinced at this time that the events do not appear to represent a fabrication or hoax in the form of scale modeling. An actual field event seems to be unfolding in the video segments. It would appear unlikely that the photographer just happened onto the scene with at least six packs of Polaroid film (assuming there in fact exists 60 Polaroid prints of the scene as inferred from Guardian's documents) and a field production quality video camera accompanied by the requisite power source equipment. Subsequent field investigation supported this conclusion due to sight limitations in surrounding topography.

In spite of the quality of the camera, the photographer does not appear to be experienced with the equipment. It should also be noted that there is no evidence that the source sender of the written and video materials is the photographer. It is surprising that no tripod was used, rarely are cameras of that quality carried without the optional use of a tripod.

The disc appears to be active throughout all segments and is static (not moving relative) to the environment. The disc is not on a perfect horizontal plane to the camera but is tilted slightly rising to approximately five degrees on the right side. This position might be a product of the topography of the terrain where the disc appears to be resting.

The appearance of the disc could be likened to an upside down frying pan without the handle and with a conical shaped turret at the center top. It has vertical ridges or protruding flange elements at equidistant intervals around and extending beyond the leading edge of the disc. The underside appears to be quite hot in terms of light temperature. There should be significant evidence of physical effects relative to this light frequency phenomenon at the landing site where this event occurred.

Initial evaluation of the entity images on the video and other photographic material suggested that it might be easy to fake such images using a protective fencing or hockey face mask and black jumpsuit costuming. If the entity images were faked however, a dichotomy in logic would exist if in fact the video of the disc is authentic. A more intensive analysis of the entity images detected obvious changes in facial features that are not consistent with the mask hypothesis. And the apparent self luminosity characteristic infers a strange complexity associated with the images that would have to border on a Hollywood level make-up job.

## The Field Investigation

Satisfied that the video segments of an active landed disc were potentially authentic, the next step was to attempt to locate the exact site where the event occurred. The map that Guardian supplied did not identify the specific site where the disc landed, but did narrow the scope to an area of approximately four square miles. On May 9, 1992 I arranged to meet several field investigators from the Toronto based Canadian UFO Research Network (CUFORN) at a prearranged location in Carleton Place not far from the area outlined on Guardian's map. Graham Lightfoot, who had conducted one of the investigations at the area based on Guardian's 1989 report, agreed to be our local guide.

That first day was spent mostly trying to get a feel for the area and unsuccessfully attempting to locate a radar site depicted on Guardian's map. Using various magnetic compass devices we attempted to locate magnetic Matrix lines drawn on Guardian's map. Most of the area that we searched was heavily wooded bush country much of which was under a foot or less of water, typical Canadian swamp land. The team had split up into three groups by day's end and eventually regrouped at a restaurant in Carp some fifteen miles away from the search area. My son and I had decided to venture deep into the forest swamp attempting to locate evidence of the 1989 landing event previously reported by Guardian and hoping to find a clearing in the woods large enough to accommodate the video tape landing of 1991.

We were fortunate enough to find our way out of the swamp about an hour before dark. The other teams had left notes on the windshield of my truck with directions to the restaurant. Although we were unable to find any evidence of the events reported in 1989, we did locate an area whose topography appeared capable of containing the sequence of events depicted in the 1991 landing video tape.

Following dinner discussions, the rather large contingent from Toronto had to make the return trip back home that night and were unable to pursue further involvement in the field investigation. Having narrowed the search to the clearing we discovered that evening, Graham Lightfoot returned the next morning to join us in visiting the property owners to ask for permission to inspect the lower field. The clearing area I had seen the day before from an opening in the swamp area was surrounded by tree lines on three sides and invisible from nearby roadways as the property sloped up to a higher elevation. The residence overlooking the lower fields was situated at the crest of a rolling hillside which sloped steeply back down to the main roadway. We called on the owners at mid-morning that Sunday and met Mrs. Labenek and her three children. Dr. Labenek was toiling away on the riding mower cutting the vast expanse of grass on the front hillside and was unaware of our arrival at the time.

Graham Lightfoot reintroduced himself to Mrs. Labenek whom he'd met more than a year earlier during his investigation of the 1989 Guardian report. Mrs. Labenek had been one of the three witnesses along that sparsely populated stretch of roadway who confirmed the sighting of an unusual bright light hovering over the swamp area in 1989. We asked Mrs. Labenek if she'd seen anything unusual down in the field the previous summer. Her uneasiness with the question was quite evident as she reluctantly suggested that there was a bright light over the field, but hesitated a t giving any further details recounting the subtle ridicule, she received from giving testimony on the subject she observed over the swamp in 1989. Not wanting to press the issue at that time, we requested permission to inspect the lower field which was granted without hesitation.

It was apparent that at one time the property was broken up into three separate fields with the remnants of stone pilings for fence posts leaving mute testimony. The fields extend 2,000 feet from the crest of the hill where the residence stands to the tree line which is fenced off from the back edge of the property. The lower field is a valley which in May was quite soft with about three inches of water covering approximately thirty percent of the surface area. Much of the field was covered in dense two feet high bush grasses and generously populated with hardy juniper bushes and a few small saplings. Spring growth was just coming up all over the area. Looking for evidence of the flares activity, my thoughts were that if this was the site, there should be some remnants of the slag from the red pyrotechnics unless flare pots were used. It figured that if we could find even microscopic evidence of the pyrotechnics activity, then it should be easy through laboratory analysis to determine if the event could possibly have been a secret military operation.

Much to my surprise it was unbelievably hot under the May sunshine in Canada that day as we hauled the video camera case and other photographic equipment and sample retrieval supplies down into the field. We were immediately drawn to an area in the middle of the lower field that seemed to be devoid of the dense growth pattern common to the rest of the field. As we scouted this area it was immediately apparent that something very unusual had occurred there affecting a roughly circular pattern approximately fifty feet in diameter.

All of the plant life in this one local area appeared to have been subjected to some level of microwave frequency exposure. The grass plants had all of the pigment bleached out and were completely dehydrated but not scorched. Outside that area the same species had turned brown through natural perennial cycles. Some of these bleached white colored grass plants had strange black sooty deposits on the surface which we collected along with unaffected control samples. Subsequent laboratory analysis proved the deposits to be of Titanium residue which was not indigenous to the site and not of any known pyrotechnics mix.

More than a dozen juniper bushes were found inside the circumference of the affected area. All had evidence of gross wilting, total loss of foliage and total dehydration. It appeared as though the cellulose had been softened allowing gravity to force the plants to lie flat on the ground, apparently at which time they became quickly dehydrated and brittle. Just outside the affected area were numerous healthy juniper shrubs that stood in stark contrast to the barren waste only several feet away.

Although all of the plant life within the circle had perished due to some form of exposure, the effects were apparently not permanently toxic to the soil. Spring growth of various forms was already beginning to sprout in the affected area. No evidence of the flare activity was ever found at the site in any of the several dozen samples taken from the entire field on two expeditions for that explicit purpose.

Developing lines of sight from the affected circle area, it became evident that while the event was clearly in plain view of the Labenek residence, the neighboring properties had an obstructed view of the area due to the specific topography and surrounding tree line. Since the Guardian video showed specific changes in elevation on approach to the event, we were able to limit the angles of view and camera orientation of objects visible in the video. Locating the direction from which the camera video taped the event would prove useful in comparing subsequent eyewitness testimony.

Discovering the actual landing site would not in itself Prove that the video tape depicted an authentic alien landing operation, but decreased the possibility of a simple staged event. The extraordinary gross physical effects suggested that a significant event had occurred involving a vehicle of high technology. If the event was the result of some top secret military aircraft, there existed no evidence whatsoever to support even an attempt to clean it up. There were no vehicle tracks in the area, no latent footprints in the soggy ground and no evidence of military pyrotechnics all of which should have been easily detectable. Clearly the site had not been touched in the nine months since the event occurred.

After our preliminary field investigation we stopped back at the house up on the hill to call on Mrs. Labenek once again before leaving the area with our equipment and samples for analysis. Convinced that an actual event had occurred on the Labenek property, we informed Mrs. Labenek that a video tape of the event had been taken. We asked if she had ever heard of the name Guardian to which she genuinely seemed uninformed. The fact that a video tape of the event existed appeared to set her more at ease and she began to open up to us about what she had seen that night in August of 1991.

She was just putting her three young children to bed and had walked into her upstairs bedroom where the windows provide a panoramic view of the lower field. There was no need for privacy shades which would only spoil the rustic view. As Mrs. Labenek crossed the room, she couldn't help but see the bright flicker of red fires deep in the field below. She went to the window and threw up the sash for a closer look. She said there was a lot of smoke and a lot of light from the cherry red fires but they didn't seem to be catching the brush or moving toward the forest swamp area and so she hesitated about calling the fire department so late on a Sunday night. There was a substantial fine for calling in false alarms and she sensed that they might burn themselves out before the fire trucks could arrive so she stayed at the open window to keep a close watch.

The Labenek boys were watching from their bedroom on the opposite end of the house while Dr. Quarrington, living in the house next door, was sitting in his den watching television when he saw what appeared to be red lightning over the Labenek field next door. He got up to go to the window to investigate but could only see the flickering glow of red light over the horizon from his vantage point. As he stepped outside to investigate further, he saw a tremendously bright elliptical white light with a golden aura descending over the trees out of his view into the Labenek field.

Mrs. Labenek and her two boys were independently watching from the upstairs windows as the disc shaped object moved over top of the red fires and settled to about ten feet above the ground in front of and to the right of the red flare like fires. There was no sound except for the barking of a dog(s) and none of these witnesses could see any movement of people in the field. There was so much light coming from the craft that it was easy to define it's structural shape which was highlighted by a bright flashing blue light on top which luminated a cone shaped central hump on the disc shaped object. After several minutes the object began to rise and then disappeared as if someone had turned off a light switch.

Meanwhile on an opposing side of the field through a short stand of trees, Sarah Janille's (pseudonym) dog began excitedly pacing back and forth from an open living room window to the den where she was watching television. When the dog began barking at the front window, Sarah got up to go check on the disturbance. As she peered through the open window, she noticed a peculiar array of red lights glowing through the trees across the street which she assumed were fireworks in the Labenek field. As she continued to watch, she saw a set of colored lights rise up over
As she peered through the open window, she noticed a peculiar array of red lights glowing through the trees across the street which she assumed were fireworks in the Labenek field. As she continued to watch, she saw a set of colored lights rise up over

the treetops and angle off at about forty five degrees before instantly vanishing. After waiting a while to see if there would be more, she returned to the den to ponder the event. She thought it was strange that the fireworks didn't make any sound and didn't explode into an umbrella of light like normal fire- works displays.

Out of curiosity she decided to venture outside onto her driveway to catch a closer look. Suddenly just above the trees in front of her was a most awesome sight of swirling colored lights which defined a strange looking object like nothing she'd ever seen before. As the object descended in front of her, she almost collapsed in panic attempting to retreat closer to the house. The Labenek dogs could be heard barking up a storm in the distance.

While the cylindrical object hovered, two occupants whose skin glowed a yellowish white came out of the vehicle and opened a panel on the side exposing a tremendous amount of white light. As the one "pig nosed" entity worked at the open panel, the other motioned sort of a hurry up signal as he pointed over the roof of Sarah's house. She recalled feeling quite concerned as the creature struggled to close the panel on the side of the craft and seemed to be moving as though in water or molasses in trying to reboard. The next thing she remembered was being back on the couch startled at the roaring sound of a helicopter bearing down low over the roof of her house. In a somewhat groggy state she ran back to the window, but could only hear the helicopter hovering and flying around the Labenek field. She was relieved that it didn't crash into the trees across the street.. Weeks later she recalled in explicit detail being on board the craft he called a car with it's headlights turned off racing by in front of her house just after the helicopter flew over the trees descending into the Labenek field. Perhaps it was Guardian fleeing the area and trying not to be detected.

Following a well documented pattern of helicopter harassment activity of the witnesses at the site, an investigation of the origin of the helicopters was launched with the cooperation of the Canadian Department of National Defence. The publicly stated conclusion by DND was that the helicopters did not originate from Canada. That conclusion has been debated by other Canadian Agencies whose investigations suggested that DND was more aware of the situation than what was publicly acknowledged.

## Some Final Conclusions

What actually happened in the fields of West Carleton? Was it an elaborately staged hoax? Was it some kind of Top Secret military vehicle landing on private property? Or was it powerful evidence of visitation by beings of non-human origin? Since witnesses have agreed to take polygraph exams, we can probably eliminate them from complicity in any hoax hypothesis. NBC's "Unsolved Mysteries" Production Company invested between $115,000 and $250,000 attempting to recreate the events depicted in the Guardian video yet were unable to meet the criteria. Even NASA's Jet Propulsion Laboratory optical film analyst Dr. Robert Nathan was unable to find any evidence of a hoax related to the video. Therefore we can comfortably set aside even an elaborate hoax hypothesis as an answer for these events.

The lack of any physical evidence at the site of the flare or pyrotechnics activity became the single biggest mystery in the case investigation. Video analysis eliminated the possibility of misinterpretation of the pyrotechnics activity as camouflaged electrical lighting with companion cosmetic smoke canisters. According to top experts in pyrotechnics chemistry, there would be no way to hide or extract the long term residual effects of the primary pyrotechnic residue ingredients pouring over the field in the form of smoke from the red flare activity. There- fore we can conclude that whatever form of pyrotechnics used during the event, they do not conform to known military or any human known compounds that academicians say would be required for red colored flare type pyrotechnics. Added to the gross physical evidence of Titanium residue from the craft, the apparent microwave exposure of the plants, the helicopter response and eyewitness verification confirming the exact location of the site, this pyrotechnics mystery would appear to be the smoking gun UFO researchers have been in search of for decades.

Few conclusions can be drawn about the enigmatic anonymity known publicly as Guardian. Did he too befall the same fate as Sarah when the blue beam from the craft was pointed at the camera? Our investigation has located a strong suspect as to Guardian's identity. There appears to be absolutely no evidence to suggest that Guardian has distorted the facts in any way. His choice to remain anonymous has gratefully forced us to focus on the evidence presented instead of challenging his credibility. It seems most UFO investigations tend to focus so much attention on the level of veracity and motives of the messenger that we often misplace our objective priorities. In this case the scientific analyses have proven to be the real tools of investigation. Nonetheless, our thirst for answers to the Guardian mystery will remain unquenched until he at least anonymously can fulfill the myriad of inquiries about his knowledge of the event and the entities he apparently encountered.

## The Aftermath

As I prepare to return to West Carleton Township for the seventh time in this expanding investigation, more evidence has surfaced with regard to the apparent alien presence there. On February 10th following the local broadcast of "Unsolved Mysteries", another sighting was reported on the same property. The event apparently completely overwhelmed an elderly lady who had not witnessed any of the previous events. And again on may the 12th of this year at 8:30 PM just before dark, another report came in. This time a red-orange disc hovering directly over the previous landing spot lifted off slowly and instantly vanished upon clearing the treetops in the field below. There has been talk of an alien camp nearby and helicopters that descend into the forest where no roads have been found to access. Further still there are claims of strange looking footprints along the banks of a nearby stream. And so the investigation will continue...

Weird diagrams and papers were also included in the mail that
Oechsler received from an individual calling himself The Guardian.

# VANISHING MIB – GHOSTS OR TELEPORTATION? BY TIM SWARTZ

The author is one of the top investigators of the paranormal today. He has been a guest on Coast to Coast AM as well as numerous other programs. In addition to his work in the UFO and metaphysical fields he has also operated as a TV and movie producer. He is editor of the weekly on line version of www.ConspiracyJournal.com

At the time of the incidents in 1980, Maria Korn was a 14-year-old boarder at the Convent of Jesus and Mary in Milton Keynes, Buckinghamshire, Great Britain. As reported by researcher Robert Bull, Maria was receiving psychological counseling from a Dr Black for acute anorexia and sleeping difficulties.

One night Maria couldn't sleep and got up, at about 1:00 AM to look at the stars. She stood by the window overlooking the tennis court and was surprised to see a large, ball-shaped flashing light inside the tennis court itself, which was completely surrounded by wire netting. She looked at it for about five minutes, then turned away. When she looked again at about 1:30 AM the object had gone, but she heard a strange whirring sound and, looking up, she saw the object again just above the window, but there were no lights on it this time. The object then moved off rapidly.

Tim Swartz is consider one of the top researchers today.

The next morning, none of the other girls mentioned having seen anything strange during the night, and Maria kept her experience to herself. Later that morning she was playing tennis when she slipped and fell, and was surprised to see a large, shallow, circular depression seemingly burnt onto the tennis court, exactly where she had seen the object the night before. The next day the police arrived to inspect the damage, but Maria didn't tell anyone what she had seen two nights before.

Three or four months later Maria was in a math class when one of the nuns, Sister Jennifer, interrupted the class and took her out, saying that she had a visitor. Maria thought at the time that it was unusual for the class to be interrupted, visitors normally came only at weekends, and she was worried in case the visitor was bringing bad news. Sister Jennifer showed her into a dining room where, sitting at a large table, was not one visitor but two men dressed in black. The heat was on and the room felt warm as Maria entered it, but as soon as she saw the two men she felt cold, and she put on the jacket that she was carrying.

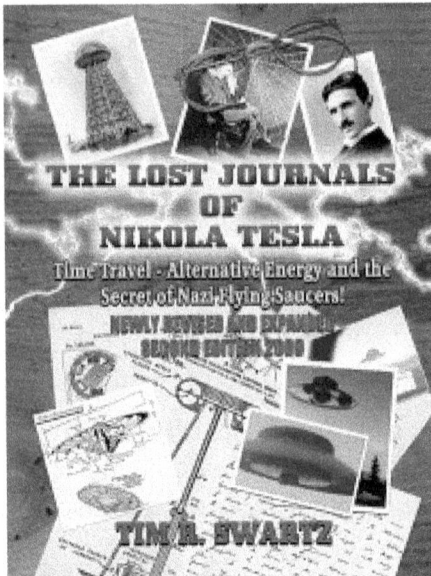

The Lost Journals of Nikola Tesla is Tim Swartz's all time best seller.

Maria had never seen her visitors before, and she asked them who they were. They told her they were with Dr Black, her psychiatrist. She stared at their eyes, which weren't brown or blue, but a strange brownish grayish color. She found the experience frightening, and looked away.

The men asked her how she was and how she was doing at school, just a normal, polite conversation. As they talked Maria noticed several other strange things about her visitors. They looked the same, as if they were identical twins, their skin was smooth and featureless, no beard and no sign that they ever needed to shave at all. Their hair was shiny black, each brushed in the same style and not a hair out of place, their black suits, seemingly brand new, fitted perfectly as if tailor-made and having razor-sharp creases. Their ties and socks were also black, exactly the same black as their trousers and jackets. One of the men then asked Maria if anything strange had happened at the convent recently. She instantly thought that they must mean what she had seen at the tennis court – but she was afraid to admit anything she knew to the strangers, so she said no. The two men obviously knew she was lying as they continued to press the question. Just then the school lunchtime bell rang. The man asked what the bell was for, then told Maria she had better go to lunch, adding that they had to leave.

Although the men looked to be like businessmen, they didn't appear to be wearing watches as one of them asked Maria the time. The men had been drinking coffee during their talk with Maria, but when she shook hands with them as she was saying goodbye she noticed that their hands were ice cold, despite the fact that they had been holding hot cups of coffee during most of the conversation.

One of the men asked Sister Jennifer if Maria could show them the way out, saying finally that: "we'll be back to see you again." She walked to the doorway and was amazed to see that the two men were walking and swinging their arms exactly in step with each other.

They walked outside to their waiting black car, Maria noticing as they did so that, although it was a windy day, their hair didn't move, as if it was glued down. The car had a chauffeur, also dressed in black, who must have been waiting all this time. As the car moved off Maria noticed that the number plate had white characters on a black background, which she thought was strange. It also had mirror windows; Maria couldn't see through the windows into the car, but she thought that the men could see out. She caught a glimpse into the car when one of the men opened a door, but all she could see was black, no seats, and no dashboard. It was as if she was looking into a black hole. The car moved off silently. There was no sound of an engine being started, no exhaust fumes. (An electric car?) She was also mystified that although she saw the car turn out of the convent gate, she didn't see it moving up the hill that led to the convent. It had completely disappeared on the only road leading to the convent.

Maria stood where she was for several minutes, unable to move. She could hear Sister Jennifer calling to her, but she couldn't turn around and go to her. Sister Jennifer asked her if she was all right, at which point she "snapped out of it" and was able to move again.

She asked Maria who the men were and Maria replied, saying that they were from Dr Black; although they were both surprised that Dr Black hadn't warned them that the men would be coming. When, a few weeks later, Maria saw Dr Black, she asked her about her visitors. Dr Black said she hadn't sent the men, and would never send anyone without informing Maria first.

UFO and Paranormal researcher, Tim Swartz, seen here taking a break after visiting the Kings Chamber at the Great Pyramid in Egypt. Swartz has visited most of the existing wonders of the ancient world, but is most happy home with his wife, two cats and dog shadow.

Although Maria never saw her MIBs again, she did begin to develop psychic powers and have extraordinary experiences. While still at the convent she: Bent a spoon, Uri Geller style – Timed herself swimming under water for five minutes before surfacing – She had an out-of-body experience. Experienced an upsurge in her creative and academic abilities, tested and verified by Dr Black. Most amazingly of all, she also claimed that on one occasion, at night, she went out into the convent yard and began to fly. This was witnessed by several other girls, who ran around trying to catch her when she flew low enough.

After Maria left the convent her strange experiences and abilities continued. She found that she could make things disappear and reappear by just thinking about them. She could make light bulbs burn out; she started a stalled car engine (with a jammed starter motor and a totally dead battery) just by willing it. She claimed to be able to turn red traffic lights to green, repeatedly, even after they had just changed to red. Strangely enough, Maria also experienced several episodes where she was unexpectedly teleported over the distance of several miles. Once, she stepped out of her front door to get the mail and found herself standing on the sidewalk in a neighborhood over five miles from her home. This happened without any warning and, as far as she could tell, was instantaneous. Marie can offer no explanation on why these strange events have centered on her.

Many of the things that happened to her were witnessed by others and were undoubtedly real. The UFO she saw left a depression and burn marks on the ground which was there for all to see; her MIBs were seen by other people and they drank

their coffee; her spoon bending, the increase in her academic and artistic abilities, light-bulb popping, some teleportation incidents, UFO sightings and other events can all be testified to.

In another weird case, also in Great Britain, Mrs. Evans (pseudonym) of Portsmouth, Hampshire went to visit the local grocer's store one morning in the autumn of 1977. In the shop she saw a tall man, dressed in black. He was ahead of her, so she stood back to wait until he was served.

As she stood in line Mrs. Evans noticed that the man's gaze was fixed upon her. She found this unnerving; he looked at her as if he knew her, as if he had been expecting her. He left the store when it was her turn at the cash register.

When she left the shop, Mrs. Evans noticed that the man was standing nearby, as if waiting for someone. As she started to walk, he began walking also, keeping five or six paces ahead of her. As she watched him she began to form the impression that he was "unusual," although she couldn't say just why.

Mrs. Evans was half-way home when he turned left into a side road. As she crossed the road, she looked to her left out of curiosity only to see the same person standing in the middle of the road. Facing her now, their eyes met once more. He nodded three times, without any change in his facial expression. His gaze was intense and penetrating. Then, to Mrs. Evans's utter amazement; he vanished without moving from the spot, "like someone turning out a light."

Thoroughly unnerved by now, she hurried home later recalling several strange things about the man:

* His clothes looked brand new, as though they had only just been bought. He was dressed from head to foot in black (except for his white shirt).

* His skin was albino-type white, as was his hair, which was wispy. His eyes were jet black, and he appeared to be in his early 50s, but there were no wrinkles on his skin, and no sign of any facial hair or stubble.

*He had unusually broad shoulders, a narrow waist, and he walked upright with a stiff gait. There seemed to be no natural curve to his spine, which was seemingly perfectly straight.

This was not Mrs. Evans only encounter with the unusual; in 1979, over a year after her original MIB encounter. In her kitchen one day, she became aware that there was a figure standing beside her. Her husband walked in and shouted: "Who's that? What's he doing here?" Whereupon the figure, which did not seem to be totally solid, ran out of the open kitchen door and disappeared.

On another occasion, Mrs. Evans was returning home one evening when she saw, in the light from a street lamp, a tall figure. The figure was completely black and seemed to be wearing some kind of helmet, making her think of a scuba diver. At this moment her husband walked out of the front door and again shouted: "Who's that? What's he doing here?" He was convinced by now that this was Mrs. Evans's secret lover.

As her husband shouted, and as their dog started to bark, the figure glided forward, going through her neighbor's front garden hedge. She later recalled that the figure appeared at first to be completely solid and real, but it grew more transparent and eventually vanished as it slowly went through the bushes.

On another day, in broad daylight, Mrs. Evans encountered a "strange little man" who appeared in front of her and walked on by. On turning around, expecting to see his back, she was shocked to find that he had vanished.

She described the man as small, about five feet tall, olive skinned, large, round dark eyes, and black hair, slicked straight back. He seemed to be wearing some kind of RAF uniform except that it looked made-to-measure, perfectly cut and stitched. His shoes looked brand new but were not the current fashion. He walked towards her with his arms held up in front of him, gazing straight ahead with blank eyes.

On yet another occasion, again in daylight, Mrs. Evans was out walking, and she came upon a small van parked in the road. The van was white, with what looked like blue clouds and flowers painted on it. As she approached the van, its door suddenly opened and a little person jumped down in front of her. She just kept slowly walking as she and the little person gazed at each other.

At first she thought she was seeing a doll, or puppet wearing a checkered shirt and blue jeans, but she was startled as she looked into his eyes, which were jet black, marble-like, with two white dots where the pupils should have been.

He seemed to have Eskimo features, with dull black, dead straight hair, roughly cut in a pageboy style. He seemed to have a knowing look in his eyes, which disturbed her. As he passed by her she tried to look over her shoulder to see him, but her neck did not seem to be moving normally and she could only see him out of the corner of her eye.

Mrs. Evans thought he seemed to be a freak of some kind, although he was perfectly proportioned. In this case and others, it was the eyes that made her realize that she was not seeing something normal.

Another encounter came one evening in Mrs. Evans's front garden. She noticed movement within a large bush that was in the garden; as if a cat or other small animal was inside it. She remembers that everything seemed unnaturally still and quiet. Slowly, the bush began to part in two or three places. Instead of the cat that she was expecting, she was amazed to see faces, seemingly those of children. When she realized that these were not children, she froze, and the hairs on the back of her neck stood up on end. She began to hear soft clucking sounds, the sort of noise one makes when trying to make friends with a shy animal.

What she saw made her think of elves, pixies and the like. They did not seem to be totally solid looking and the bushes covered their lower bodies. As their misshapen hands extended out towards her she decided that she had seen enough and ran indoors. As she ran upstairs her husband called out to her, asking if she had seen what it was that had just bolted out of the front garden. Later, with her heart still fluttering, she came down and looked nervously outside. The "elves" were gone, but she saw, walking towards her down the path near her home, a dark figure lit by an aura that moved with it. Before it suddenly disappeared, Mrs. Evans saw that the figure had short, dark curly hair and a pointy face with very high cheekbones. Its eyes seemed to glow as it stared at her in a menacing way.

Like others who have had similar experiences, Mrs. Evans found herself undergoing a whole series of unexplainable occurrences. As a young girl in 1947, there was a poltergeist in the family home, although she herself did not realize this and her parents who had never even heard of the poltergeist phenomenon did not tell her about it until many years later.

October 16, 1973 - her father sees a massive UFO. Winter 1977/Spring 1978 – Mrs. Evans sees (with her husband) her first UFO. Christmas 1978 - early New Years 1979 - UFOs, hauntings, poltergeists. Her husband and neighbors also experience these phenomena, but her house seems to be the focus. She begins to notice strange marks, burns, bruises, and puncture marks on her skin, which seem to appear in the mornings after restless nights. Mrs. Evans reports seeing "about a dozen" UFOs from Christmas 1978 to November 1979.

A blood-like substance appeared "out of thin air" at her home, also a "transparent, jelly-like" substance. Strong smells – she, her husband and her neighbor saw a small, yellowish cloud, accompanied by a strong smell of sulphur. On another occasion there was a strong, "overpowering" smell of incense, also smells of zoo animals' cages and wet animal fur. On two occasions when "something unusual" passed over her head, she felt a click, or tap, on her temples, somewhat like a tiny electric shock.

Things appeared and disappeared in her home: keys, jewelry, eye glasses. Her purse rose from the table, flew through the air and landed in her left hand. The teakettle whistled as if boiling, but there was no water in it, and the gas was not turned on. Flames came out of fingernails, which turned bright turquoise overnight, the color being on the underside of the nail.

A "paper tape streamer" appeared out of nowhere and flew through the air in her living room. It bore the words: "Don't be afraid - we are coming back in October." Her milkman saw her standing at her front door and waved to her, and then he turned around and saw her walking down the street towards him. Other people reported seeing her at various other places when she was actually miles away.

In an article titled: "MIB Activity Reported From Victoria B.C.", (Flying Saucer Review, January 1982) Dr. P.M.H. Edwards, formerly professor of linguistics at the University of Victoria, detailed an unusual case of MIB teleportation.

In October 1981, three days after a UFO sighting in Victoria, British Columbia, Grant Breiland saw two sun-tanned expressionless men who lacked fingernails observing him at a K-Mart department store. They were stiff, seemingly "at attention," and were dressed in very dark blue clothes. They approached, and one asked Breiland in a monotonous, mechanical voice, "What is your name?" Their lips did not move when they spoke.

Breiland said, "I'm not going to tell you that."

The other man asked where Breiland lived, and then, "What is your number?"

Breiland did not respond. The two strange men stared at him for a few seconds, then turned and left, but Breiland followed them out of curiosity. The two men waited at the edge of a muddy, plowed field and, as Breiland watched them, he thought he heard someone call his name. Turning around, he saw no one. The two men walked into the field, and again, Breiland thought that he heard someone call out his name. Suddenly, the two men vanished three-quarters of the way across the field. Checking around, Breiland was unable to locate any footprints in the muddy field. It was as if the two men were ghosts.

Breiland noted that, mysteriously, no other persons were in sight at the busy shopping area during the entire incident, and the setting was only repopulated after the strange men had vanished. The "depopulation" anomaly has been noted in other UFO and MIB cases, and has been termed the "Oz effect" by British UFO researcher Jenny Randles. This zone of unreality seems to indicate that these incidents could be paranormal in nature.

A "MAN IN BLACK IN TRAINING" PHOTOGRAPHED AT THE NATIONAL UFO CONFERENCE, CHARLOTTESVILLE, WVA '69

This is Tim Beckley's "famous" photo of an MIB. The "out of place" figure can be seen standing in the doorway of a building next to where Jack and Mary Robinson, a husband and wife UFO research team, were living during a wave of creature sightings circa 1965.

# SMILE MIB – YOUR ON "CANDID CAMERA"

I can't help but believe that when you take matters into your own hands and reverse the tables on them that the MIB will make a quick exit. While they do have untold capabilities to menace and perhaps even maim, at times they also seem unnecessarily timid. It is of course possible, as we have begun to realize through the pages of this study guide on the men in black, that the MIB are of various kinds. Some are secret agents of a known – or unknown – government, while others appear to be a visitor in their own right. I myself believe that the MIB are interdimensional, and are not rooted in our reality. Some might be here drawn to our world without knowing why or how to exit.

I know in the case where I photographed an MIB while in the company of Jim Moseley, he was never again seen in the neighbor in Jersey City where he had been plunked down like a zombie keeping watchful tabs on the apartment building where Jack and Mary Robinson lived.

Jim and I drove over from Manhattan without alerting the Robinson's to the fact that we were coming just in case the entire episode was being made up or fantasized by the couple. This way we could catch them off guard. Will the MIB was there just as they claimed it would be. Moseley was driving while I was in the passenger seat. Jim handed me the camera and without making a comment I took a photo of this individual hovering in the doorway along with a black car parked at the curb. Because there was traffic behind us and we wanted to park to quiz the person dressed in black we drove around the block. When we returned the individual in dark clothing was gone along with any type of car resembled anything the MIB would want to drive.

T.Allen Greenfield    Tim Beckley

Greenfield VS Beckley for who has the best MIB photo.

He was never seen again. Vanished completely out of Jack and Mary Robinson's lives.

The only other attempt I know to take a photograph of a MIB involved a long time acquaintance of mine. Allen Greenfield has been thru the flying saucer mill. He's seen and just about heard it all. Allen has edited various publications on and off since his teenage years, has organized UFO conferences in his neck of the woods. He has also been on just about every radio and tv station known to mankind that caters to believers in the paranormal. This is his little story.

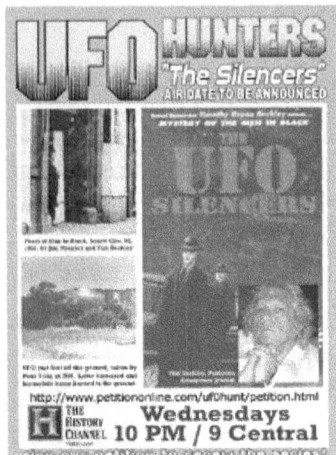

Unofficial promotional poster used to stur up a bit of excitement about an episode of the UFO Hunters known as The Silencers.

"The story in brief is this - during the Charleston W VA National UFO Conference - as I recall that was June 24, 1969 there was this guy shadowing the delegates. When he followed some of us to a restaurant, several of us - maybe you and Jim and Gray included (keep in mind this is tail end of the "Mothman period") were eating when this guy approached from behind and I decided to confront him. "Who are you?" I asked. "I am a man in black in training" he replied in a monotone, and went out into the street. As I recall it was a Sunday in downtown Charleston, so there was virtually no persons or traffic. I jumped up, breaking my chair in the process, ran out in front of him and he just stood facing me. I photographed him with my Yashica J-7 35mm camera using high speed B&W film. He then rounded a corner, I was maybe two seconds - tops - behind him, and, yet the street was now totally empty."

And so it goes — two MIBs caught on a cosmic "Candid Camera" for the entire world to see.

## UFO Hunters - The Silencers

# YOU

# HAVE

# BEEN

# WARNED!

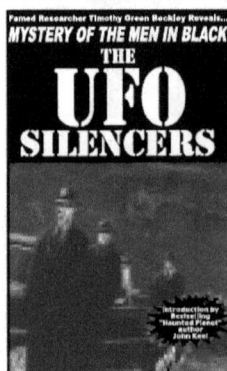

www.ingramcontent.com/pod-product-compliance
Lightning Source LLC
Chambersburg PA
CBHW062100090426
42741CB00015B/3288